From Rice Paddies and Temple Yards:
Traditional Music of Vietnam

From Rice Paddies and Temple Yards:
Traditional Music of Vietnam

Phong Thuyet Nguyen
Patricia Shehan Campbell

World Music Press

From Rice Paddies and Temple Yards:
Traditional Music of Vietnam
by
Phong Thuyet Nguyen
Patricia Shehan Campbell

All Photographs by Phong Nguyen © 1989 except for:
pages 21, 24, 49, 59, © 1989 Pham Ngoc Lanh, used by permission;
17, 23 (bottom), 77, © 1989 Timothy Tucker, used by permission; and
47 © 1989 Ken Krenick, used by permission
Cover Illustration and pages 15, 25, 39 © 1990 Thi Hop Nguyen

ISBN 0-937203-32-7 Paperback
ISBN 0-937203-33-5 Audio cassette
ISBN 0-937203-34-3 Book and Tape SET

All Rights Reserved

World Music Press
Multicultural Materials for Educators
Judith Cook Tucker, Publisher; Editor-in-Chief
PO Box 2565 Danbury CT 06813
(203) 748-1131

Original Paperback Edition
Printed in the United States of America
Music engraved by Judith Cook Tucker using Professional Composer® version 2.2
Typeset using a Macintosh® Plus, Pagemaker® and Laserwriter® Plus
Printed by the Princeton University Press on Acid-free paper.

First Printing 1990
Second Printing January, 1992 (all errors detected in first printing corrected)

Library of Congress Catalog Card Number 89-52161

Phong Thuyet Nguyen, Ph.D.

was raised in Can Tho province in the Mekong delta of South Vietnam, in a village called Tam Ngai. He was born into a musical family that played art music, music for festivals, rituals, ceremonies, Buddhist chant, chamber music and theatrical music. At the age of five, he began his musical training with his father, concentrating first on singing and progressing to instrumental instruction at age 10. His formal teacher for many years was a well-known music master in South Vietnam, Mr. Tram Van Kien (Muoi Kien), who taught him vocal and instrumental chamber, ritual and theater music, and Buddhist chant. Even as a child Dr. Nguyen performed in many provinces of South Vietnam as a singer and instrumentalist. Over the years he concentrated particularly on the *đàn tranh* zither, *đàn nguyệt* lute, and *đàn bầu* monochord. When he was ten he moved to a town called Tra On, and several years later resettled in Saigon, where he studied Western music, earned a degree in literature and philosophy from the University of Saigon and taught high school literature and private music students. He was appointed principal of the high school and from 1970-74 introduced and taught classes in Vietnamese traditional music, not previously taught in schools, and only recently offered for credit. He left Saigon in 1974.

Dr. Nguyen earned his Ph. D. in Ethnomusicology at the Sorbonne University in Paris, France, and served the National Center for Scientific Research through the mid-1980s. His research centered around various aspects of Vietnamese music, including traditional song, modal systems, and the mixture of Western and Vietnamese elements in the music of contemporary Vietnam and Vietnamese-American communities. He is now considered to be one of the two recognized exponents of Vietnamese music on the international scene. A well-known and widely respected teacher and scholar, he has trained a number of students (some of who have gone on to teach traditional Vietnamese music in Vietnam), performed on numerous recordings on the Lyrichord and other labels, directed and participated in international concerts in Asia, Europe and America, and has further contributed to the field of Ethnomusicology through his books and articles. He has been the recipient of a number of grants by the United States and French governments to aid in the collection and preservation of Vietnamese musics. Dr. Nguyen is currently on the faculty of Kent State University in Ohio.

Patricia Shehan Campbell, Ph.D.

is associate professor of music education at the University of Washington. She received her Ph. D. in music education with a concentration in ethnomusicology from Kent State University, where she studied South Indian mridangam and Karnatic vocal techniques with Ramnad V. Raghavan, played in the Thai Ensemble and studied Laotian *kaen* with Terry Miller and Jarernchai Chonpairot. Her interest in world music has taken her as student, researcher, and clinician to Bulgaria, Hungary, Japan, India and Australia. Dr. Campbell has served on the faculties of Washington University in St. Louis and Butler University in Indianapolis, where she was chair of the department of music education. While in St. Louis, she took part in an NEA-funded project resulting in *Silk Sarongs and City Streets,* a study of Laotian resettlement in the U.S. She is a consultant on music in early and middle childhood, multicultural music education, and the use of movement as a pedagogical tool. A prolific writer, she has published articles on the issues of crosscultural music learning, music preference, and methods for children in numerous journals. She is author of *Sounds of the World: Music of Southeast Asia,* and with Sam-Ang Sam, *Silent Temples, Songful Hearts: Traditional Music of Cambodia,* and co-editor of *Multicultural Perspectives in Music Education* (with William M. Anderson). She is an active member of the Music Educators National Conference, Society for Ethnomusicology, College Music Society, International Society for Music Education, Organization of Kodaly Educators, and the Dalcroze Society.

Foreword

During the past ten years we have witnessed an increasingly serious courtship between the formerly discrete fields of music education and ethnomusicology. Practitioners of music education — especially classroom teachers — have developed a heightened curiosity about musical traditions beyond those traditionally taught and at the same time recognized the increasingly diverse cultural backgrounds of their students. The practical limitations of time and place have prevented most teachers from conducting their own primary research into these "non-Western" traditions, as diverse as African, East Asian, Southeast Asian, South Asian, Middle Eastern, and Latin American. At the same time, practitioners of ethnomusicology have become aware of the need to transmit their findings to a constituency broader than fellow scholars.

The ideal solution has been to bring together someone having expertise in a specific musical tradition with someone having expertise in methodology (and not a little knowledge of the specific tradition as well). *From Rice Paddies and Temple Yards: Traditional Music of Vietnam* will surely serve as a model for further publications in a field some call "applied ethnomusicology."

Dr. Phong Nguyen is the ultimate "insider," trained in the tradition from childhood and one of the world's greatest exponents of traditional Vietnamese music. His training in scholarship at the Sorbonne has also made him an articulate spokesman for this little-known but exquisite tradition. In this work Dr. Patricia Shehan Campbell combines her expertise in music education methodology, her experience in the classroom, and her enthusiasm for Vietnamese music with Dr. Nguyen's profound knowledge to offer teachers at various levels practical material for the teaching of Vietnamese music. This work is representative of an important new trend in the way music is taught in the United States.

This work appears at an auspicious moment in history, as a new world order emerges after the long and dark years of the "cold war." The unthinkable dream becomes reality, almost on a daily basis. Vietnam has been a part of America's recent past but not the one that most wish to remember and celebrate. For Vietnamese-Americans, time has begun to heal the trauma which brought them to America, and as they have become established members of American society, they can allow themselves to remember again their Vietnamese culture as a positive attribute. As such, an interest in teaching the music of a people who have until now symbolized to us more agony than ecstasy is surely a step in the healing process.

Terry E. Miller
Professor of Ethnomusicology
Center for the Study of World Musics
Kent State University, Kent, Ohio

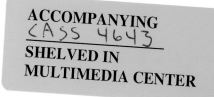

Contents

Musical Transcriptions

Illustrations

Photographs

Pronunciation Guide

Vowels:

a	ah (like "r")
ă	ah (with rising-up)
â	er (with rising-up)
e	air
ê	ay (like "day")
i	ee
o	or
ô	oh
ơ	er
u	oo (like "too")
ư	ew (like "new")
y	ee

(Note: Pronunciation is also affected by marks over vowels indicating gliding tones. These are explained in Chapter 2, page 27.)

Consonants:

	(North)	*(Central & South)*
b	b	b
c	k	k
ch	ts (strong)	ts (weak)
d	z	y
đ	d	d
gi	zee	yi
ho	hor	hw
k	k	k
l	l	l
m	m	m
n	n	n (prefix), ng (ending)
nh	nya	nya
ph	f	f
qu	kw	w
r	z	r
s	s	sh
t	t (weak)	t (weak)
th	th (strong)	th (strong)
v	v	b(ee) or y (like "yes")
x	s	s

Preface

This book-and-tape set represents the first complete resource for the introduction of Vietnamese traditional music and culture in the English language. The book unfolds in several sections. The first part consists of a thumbnail sketch of the Vietnamese people, their land, their history, and their customs, including music, so that the reader may become familiar with this people whose joys and sorrows are expressed in their songs and instrumental music. The second section presents an introduction to Vietnamese language, a description of Vietnamese traditional musical forms and instruments, and an account of changing traditions in Vietnamese-American communities within the United States. A series of twelve lessons comprise the third section, designed for the teaching of Vietnamese music, and Vietnamese culture through music. The progression of experiences suggested in each lesson will enable young people and adults, Vietnamese and non-Vietnamese, to understand the beauty and logic of Vietnamese musical traditions.

The accompanying tape provides examples of several important musical genres, including children's songs, folk songs that blend language and literature with music in their image-laden poetic verse, instrumental solo and ensemble works, and poetry that is more music than it is speech in its elaborate recitation. While the book offers an intellectual understanding of Vietnamese traditions, the heart of the culture is found in the music. The performers are all Vietnamese refugees living in the United States. Some are professional musicians, some enjoy making music in their leisure time. All sing and play in a manner that clearly reveals both the beauty inherent in this tradition and their reverence and love for it. We are deeply grateful to them for joining with us on this project. We suggest that you listen to the tape first, without explanation, and absorb the sound, texture and mood of the music. Allow the book to enhance and guide you to further understanding *after* you have been exposed to the music. The nuances of pronunciation, gliding tones and microtones, so hard to notate accurately, will become far clearer and well within reach through aural learning.

We feel this project was inevitable. Vietnamese people, many of them refugees resettled in California, Washington and Texas, and in smaller communities such as those in Ohio, Wyoming, Massachusetts and Connecticut, are looking for a guide to help retain and transmit traditional Vietnamese music and culture to Vietnamese children in community centers and Saturday morning schools. Likewise, teachers of music, the arts, history and social studies in elementary and secondary schools desperately need a resource that reveals the beauty and vitality of the music and culture of some of the newest members of their classrooms. All too often Vietnamese people have been viewed entirely through the harsh and distorted filter of the war experience. It is rare that the fundamental gentleness of the Vietnamese character is explored. People of all ages living side by side in communities of ethnic diversity need accurate information, free of stereotypes and misconceptions, to help them celebrate that diversity, rather than be suspicious of it. We both share a sense of zeal for bringing understanding of and appreciation for Vietnamese music and culture, and music *in* culture to interested students on all levels. It is our hope that *From Rice Paddies and Temple Yards: Traditional Music of Vietnam* will refresh and enrich all of our readers and listeners.

1 *"Crack your whip while roars the autumn wind"*
Historical and Cultural Background

Vietnam
and Neighboring Countries in Southeast Asia

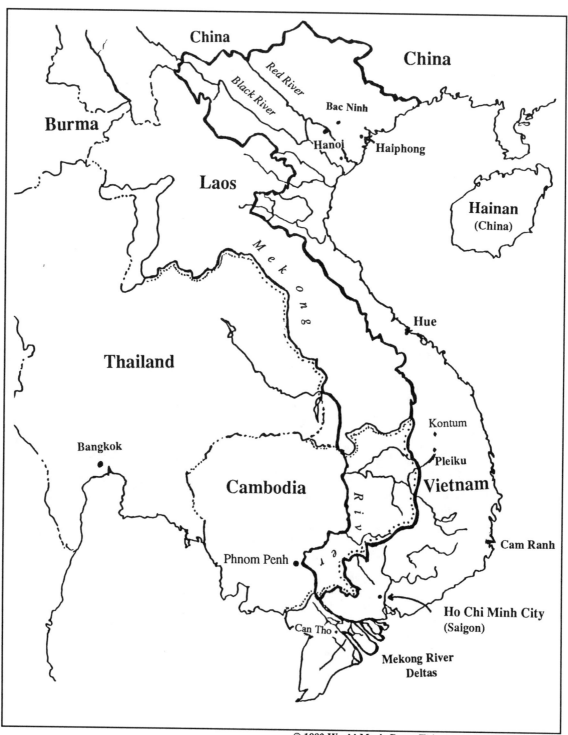

In the region referred to by geographers as Southeast Asia lies the elongated "S"- shaped country of Vietnam. Occupying an area of about 128, 408 square miles, it is directly south of China, bordered by Cambodia and Laos on the west, the Gulf of Tonkin to the northeast, the Gulf of Thailand to the southwest and the South China Sea to the east. Vietnam's strategic location has resulted in a number of international confluences through the ages.

Geography

"Two baskets of rice slung on a pole" is a description the Vietnamese offer of their country. The baskets are the deltas of the Red River in the north and the Mekong in the south, and the carrying pole of those rice baskets is a series of mountain chains along the western border, known as the Annamite Cordillera (*Trường Sơn*, "Long Mountains"). The whole is about 1000 miles long—similar to California. Vietnam can be further divided into eight natural regions: three low-lying plains (including the two major river deltas), three mountain areas, a northern midland region of terraced hills, and a large southern mountain plateau. There is little geographic unity throughout the country, but since the bulk of the 52,750,000 Vietnamese people cultivate rice, most of them are concentrated in the tiny, humid lowland pockets and along the seacoast.

Central Highlands landscape.

One half of the country is covered by jungle-like rain forests, and nearly four-fifths of the land is covered by trees and tropical vegetation. There is diversity in the lay of the land, however, from mountains and plains to lush green valleys, carefully manicured terraces, picturesque sandy beaches, flat grassy prairies, swamps, and even small pockets of desert. Vietnam is also home to many animals that roam the lush forests and swim in the full rivers and delta streams, including elephants, wild boar, oxen and deer, water buffalo, tigers, leopards, pythons, crocodiles, and great numbers of monkeys and wild birds.

Vietnam is warm and humid, and the rainy monsoon season extends from June to November. Blowing southwest from the Indian Ocean, the monsoon brings intense heat and typhoons along with heavy rains. The average yearly rainfall is fifty-nine inches —more than Miami, Florida— while Hanoi receives seventy-two inches annually. Houses of the Red and Mekong deltas are elevated on poles as an adaptation to thwart the powerful rivers that regularly overflow their banks. Networks of canals have helped to lessen the floods, and are used for irrigation in the highlands where rainfall is rare in the winter months.

Climate

Vietnam is one of the world's leading producers of rice, along with other countries of Southeast Asia. Rice fields extend over more than 12 million acres today, and have been a central part of life in Vietnam for many centuries. While the kernals provide food, the rest of the plant is utilized for making beer, wine and flour, and for providing fuel and fertilizer, and the raw materials with which to make straw mats, and garments. "A Farmer's Calendar" is a traditional Vietnamese poem that presents the phases of work and philosophy of a rice farmer:

Rice

> The twelfth moon for potato growing,
>   the first for beans, the second for eggplant.
> In the third, we break the land
>   to plant rice in the fourth while the rains are strong.
> The man plows, the woman plants,
>   and in the fifth: the harvest, and the gods are good—
>   an acre yields five full baskets this year.
> I grind and pound the paddy, strew husks
>   to cover the manure,
>   and feed the hogs with bran.
> Next year, if the land is extravagant,
>   I shall pay the taxes for you.
> In plenty or in want, there will still be you and me,
>   always the two of us.
> Isn't that better than always prospering, alone?

Vietnamese cuisine consists of rice and fish as the main ingredients, reflecting the agricultural and maritime culture. Fish and shellfish, including shrimp, lobster, and crab are common sea- and river-foods. "Oryza fatua" the first strain of rice known throughout much of the world, was found in Vietnam in the Early Stone Age (5,000 years ago). Various wild and cultivated spices from trees and bushes were traded to the Middle East as early as the first century A.D., others such as curries and hot red and black peppers were introduced by traders en route to and from India, Indonesia and China. In more modern times, French-style coffee and baked goods have been popular. Tropical fruits inlcuding melons, coconut, mango, lime and orange are cultivated, and ginger, mint, sesame, peanuts, sweet potatoes, sugar cane, basil and lemon grass are also abundant.

Other Foods

Much of Vietnam's earliest history is shrouded in folklore and legend. According to one mythical tale, the history of the Vietnamese people began with King De Minh who was descended from Chen Nong, a divine Chinese sovereign honored as the father of Chinese agriculture. De Minh traveled to the southern part of his kingdom, in present-day Vietnam, where he met an immortal woman from the mountains. De Minh married her, and they had a son named Loc Tuc who became the king of Xich-Quy, the land of the Red Devils. Loc Tuc married a sea goddess, and they had a son named Lac Long Quan, or the Dragon Lord. The reign of the Dragon Lord was a golden age, and poets through the ages referred to the Vietnamese as the "grandchildren of Lac."

Early History

The Vietnamese legends became associated with historical fact as they continued. Lac Long Quan married Au Co, the daughter of a Chinese emperor. Au Co laid 100 eggs and hatched 100 sons. The king recognized their incompatibility, and said to his wife: "I am a dragon, and you are a fairy. We cannot remain together. I will rule the lowlands with fifty sons, and you will take fifty sons into the highlands with you." Lac Long Quan's eldest son inherited his throne, founding the first Vietnamese dynasty—the Hong Bang. His kingdom was Van Lang, established in 2879 B.C.

Archeological evidence and references in later literature offer a description of a flourishing Bronze Age Culture under the Hung kings (2879-258 B.C.) when bronze drums, engraved with scenes of dance and drum ensembles, were played. A kingdom known briefly as Au Lac covered China's southernmost Kwangtung Province and northern Vietnam between 257 and 111 B.C. Chinese generals who had broken with the Chin emperors of China conquered the region, naming the area "Nam-Viet," (Southern Country of the Viet People). With the rise to power of the Han dynasty in China, the Nam-Viet were pushed slowly south into the area of present-day Vietnam. In 111 B.C., the Han dynasty succeeded in crushing the small Vietnamese state.

Although they accepted Chinese civilization, including its philosophy, character script, social customs and art of planting rice in artificially irrigated areas, the Vietnamese preserved their identity and resisted assimilation as Chinese. A series of revolts over the centuries were unsuccessful until 939 A.D., when, during the waning days of China's Tang dynasty, the Vietnamese overthrew Chinese rule. Still, China's "Smaller Dragon" was sinicized with the characteristic stamp of the mandarin way. In addition to Chinese cultural influences, Indian beliefs and culture were deeply implanted in Vietnam at the very roots of the culture–the folk level– as early as the first century B.C. Buddhism, as practiced by the traders and merchants who plied the trade routes and stopped in the villages along the coast , was especially embraced.

A.D.

Vietnam, also called Dai Viet (Great Viet Country) and Annam (a Chinese-imposed name signifying Pacified South) matured and maintained a national identity. During the Dinh, Le, Ly and Tran dynasties, known collectively as the Buddhist-influenced Golden Period of Vietnamese culture of the tenth through fourteenth centuries A.D., music and dance flourished at the royal courts. Indigenous and foreign instruments combined to form orchestras, partly to serve as accompaniment for the newly developed theater forms, including opera. Many historical and literary works of poetry were composed then and are still sung today, a testimony to the great era of nationalism which had evolved following Vietnam's independence from China.

The Vietnamese pushed further south into the Indianized state of Champa, which had been founded in 192 A.D. and extended from north of the Mekong delta to the 18th parallel, claiming the land for their teeming population. Champa's capital was the homeport for a flourishing seaborne trade, and for longstanding cultural exchanges with India. The Chams first accepted their northern neighbor's agricultural skills, but then waged and lost territorial battles with them, until in 1471 Champa was decisively defeated. By the 1600s the Chams were conquered and the boundaries of Champa disappeared as Vietnam grew into its present area. The Vietnamese continued their colonization process into Cambodia, but with the 1863 establishment of a French protectorate in Indochina (Laos, Cambodia and Vietnam), Vietnam returned to the s-shaped country of its fifteenth century boundaries.

Despite a long-established Vietnamese culture, early contact with other *French* world cultures was common. European culture was introduced into Vietnam by *Rule* French, Portuguese and Spanish missionaries beginning in the late 1500s. (Today, about 10% of the population practices Roman Catholicism, others Taoism, Confucianism and the majority, Buddhism.) French military advisors aided Vietnam in several rebellions in the late eighteenth and nineteenth centuries, and through a jigsaw puzzle of isolated and contradictory moves, French colonial rule was firmly established at the turn of the twentieth century.

French administration of Vietnam for fifty years caused rapid westernization of the society. Many Vietnamese received French-styled schooling, learned French as well as their mother tongue, and were introduced to the literature, music and arts of the West through the French occupation. The Vietnamese emperors continued to exist, surrounded by the traditional court ceremonies, but their ruling power was drastically decreased and all major acts required the signature of the resident *superieur*.

Confrontations with French political powers occurred, especially in the north. In 1930 a nationalist movement, inspired no doubt by Sun Yat-sen's success in China, staged an uprising against the French and Ho Chi Minh organized the Indochinese Communist party. After the World War II occupation of Vietnam by Japan ended, the Democratic Republic of Vietnam was declared by a communist-led revolt in Hanoi. Ho Chi Minh then led the communists in a guerilla war against the French, culminating in the defeat of the French after the siege of a major French fortress in 1954. Vietnam was then divided at the 17th parallel into two separate countries, the Communists retaining control of the north. In a pattern reminiscent of the gradual takeover of their southern Champa neighbors by the Vietnamese in the fifteenth century, northern communist forces pursued the eradication of French and foreign influences in their cities.

The United States viewed with concern the aggression of the *US* northern region in the south, supported by Russia and China, and in 1961 *Involvement* began a period of sustained aid. Ultimately, intervention begun as military advising escalated to air strikes (begun in 1964) and ground battles until United States troop deployment increased to the tune of 550,000 personnel and enormous financial involvement for the preservation of a non-communist South Vietnam (Republic of Vietnam).

A strong division of public opinion about American involvement in Vietnam led to the gradual withdrawal of troops beginning in 1969. Despite the involvement of the United States and a cease fire signed in Paris in 1973, South Vietnam and Saigon fell to the communists in 1975. The political upheavals caused more than one million to flee Vietnam on foot, in shaky vessels, and by air, and to seek asylum in Western countries, especially France, Australia, and the United States. The points of transit for these "boat people" are Thailand, Malaysia, Indonesia, Hongkong and the Philipines.

Today, "Little Saigons" (large communities of transplanted Vietnamese) are found in the United States in Orange County, Los Angeles, San Francisco, Stockton, Merced, and Fresno, California; in Gulf Coast communities of Texas and Louisiana, and in Washington

Vietnamese Communities in the U.S.

state. Smaller communities may be found in a dozen other locations including Jamaica Plain and Northampton, Massachusetts; Houston, Beaumont, and Corpus Cristi, Texas; Danbury, Bridgeport, and Hartford, Connecticut; Minneapolis, Minnesota; Chicago, Illinois; and Seattle, Washington. Their flight and resettlement, although painful, has offered hope for a renaissance of Vietnamese cultural traditions. Music, theater, dance, the visual arts poetry and literature are rich repositories of the history of a long-enduring people. A great variety of folk and festival customs, styles of casual and formal dress and the distinctive cuisine also provide a bond between those who had to leave and their heritage. Some of these cultural features can still be observed in Vietnam, while others are preserved in Vietnamese communities throughout the world. Some traditions are changing, of course, with Western influences quite naturally shaping them, but for many, the traditional songs and instrumental music are a particularly powerfully spiritual link to their ancient and brilliant past.

Phong Nguyen's sister, wearing typical contemporary clothing, viewing the family's rice paddies.

Customs and Traditions

At least three times a year, traditional festivals take place in the villages of Vietnam. *Đình* (common house) and *chùa* (Buddhist temple) are *Festivals* where ritual ceremonies, music festivals and competitive games take place.

Among the most ancient of Vietnamese holidays is the lunar New Year, marked by the *Tết* festival. *Tết* is a time for Vietnamese people to return to their birth place, to visit the tombs of their ancestors, and to reestablish ties with the extended family. Vietnamese visit temples, pay their debts, acknowledge their errors, and offer prayers for their future during the *Tết* festival. Other important festivals are associated with the seasonal activities of planting and harvesting of rice and other crops.

Music heralds the start of festivals, competitions and ceremonies. Folk songs and theater music are sometimes performed in the yard of a home, with both adults and children attending. The audience may stand or sit on the ground, making a circle at the center of which actors and actresses perform historical, legendary or love plays on straw mats. In earlier times, traditional theater used no scenery or props, so that the performers were faced with conveying their message solely through song, instrumental music, miming, and dance. Contemporary Vietnamese theater now permits the limited use of props.

Customs are interpreted in various ways, depending upon region and whether the performers are professionals or amateurs. Respect for elders, parents, and ancestors is an important Vietnamese value expressed in ways unique to different regions. Birthdays are seldom celebrated, although a milestone birthday such as sixty, seventy or eighty may be cause for festivities. One typical custom is the *hát quan họ* folk tradition of Bac Ninh province, in which antiphonal singing between the people of two villages represents the friendship that they hold. Songs are associated with various village customs, including "head-covering," "remembering parents and ancestors," "praying," and "boating" songs. Funerals and commemoration days of the dead are ritualized with music and songs, representing gratitude of the living toward the dead. Musical ensembles and individuals perform a great deal of the ritual music repertoire on these occasions.

Because of Vietnam's warm climate, most clothing is thin and light. The traditional formal dress of Vietnam is called *áo dài* meaning *Traditional* the "long dress" of both men and women. The *áo dài* dresses have *Clothing* distinctive shapes and designs for men and for women. There is also the women's folk costume called *áo tứ thân* or "four piece dress," worn when girls sing folk songs in Bac Ninh province, in North Vietnam, or during village festivals. On special occasions, people wear hats called *khan dong*, made of silk cloth. For work in fields or market, the conical woven grass hat serves well to shed sun or rain. Minority people typically wear bright colored clothes that distinguish them from ethnic Vietnamese. For most activities, Western styles suffice.

In spite of diverse racial origins, the Vietnamese today are largely an ethnically and culturally homogeneous people. The first settlers of the area may have been Mongoloid Vietnamese, called "Viet," or possibly Indonesian, Micronesian, or Polynesian peoples. The Mongoloid Vietnamese settled on the coast and in the river valleys to fish and raise crops, while most of the other, smaller groups carved out a more precarious existence in the mountains, hills and tropical forests. The mountain people, (called *Montagnards* by the French) spring from the various Austro-Indonesian groups. The Vietnamese possessed their own language and culture from the earliest times, and they retained their own identity even when conquered and governed by the Chinese and French. Many Vietnamese resemble their northern Chinese neighbors in physical appearance, having probably descended from them or a common ancestor. Today, the ethnic minority that comprises the mountain people consists of fifty-three groups, or 13.5% of the population. They share the spirit of nationalism and honor in their claim to Vietnamese citizenry.

Ethnic Makeup

Ethnic minority group members in traditional clothing. (left to right) Lolo, Pupeo, Lachi, Laha, Colao.

Montagnard village.

Fruit vendors at an open air market in the suburbs outside of Saigon.

A temple yard in North Vietnam.

2 *From Speech to Song:*

Vietnamese Musical Form and Instruments

Đàn t'rưng bamboo xylophone of the Bahnar, an ethnic people of the Central Highlands. It is slung like a hammock on a frame. The bamboo tubes have holes in the bottom of varying lengths.

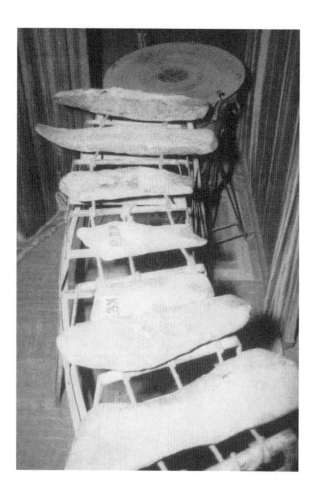

A bronze drum (top background) and a set of lithophone (stone) chimes.

Traditional Vietnamese culture includes the use of a spoken and a formal, literate language. The spoken Vietnamese language is linked to the Austro-Asiatic family. It fuses Cambodian, Thai and Chinese elements, reflecting the mixed background of the Vietnamese people. There are six tones placed within equal, high and low levels, making the language rich with varied pitches. A classic example is the word *ma*, of which there are six forms with various tones and meanings: **Language**

Phonetic Chart: "Gliding Tones"

Tonality is indicated in written Vietnamese by diacritical marks. This chart shows how the word *ma* changes in meaning as a result of changing tonality.

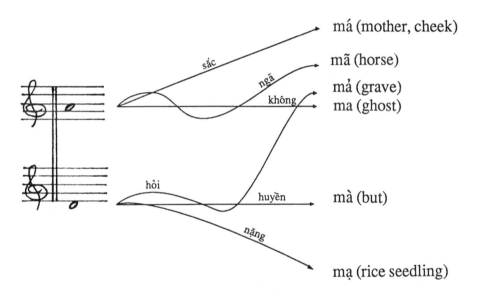

má (mother, cheek)

mã (horse)

mả (grave)
ma (ghost)

mà (but)

mạ (rice seedling)

Spoken Vietnamese sounds much like a melody with its many intoned syllables. The loud recitation of a poem can easily generate a song. In this way, long poems consisting of hundreds or thousands of phrases that are read may appear to be sung. These poems and stories are performed in various styles for entertainment. One such poem, "A Soldier's Wife," is included in this book and on the accompanying recording (*see lesson 12*).

Vietnamese literature may be found in both oral and written forms. The written literature is cast in three kinds of languages: *chữ hán* or Chinese characters, *chữ nôm* or Sino-Vietnamese characters, and *chữ quốc ngữ* or Romanized characters. *Chữ hán* was the language of higher education and the government for nearly two thousand years, while *chữ nôm* was invented during the Ly dynasty (1009-1225 A.D.) for use in vernacular literature. *Chữ quốc ngữ* which is now the official written language of Vietnam, is an exceptional case in Asia. Roman characters, first introduced to Vietnam by European Catholic missionaries in the seventeenth century were combined with Portuguese, Italian and Greek elements, making a perfect adaptation for the diacritical marks and the spelling of the language.

The nature of speech has remained an important factor in Vietnamese traditional music. The linguistic inflection which subtlely rises and falls in pitch has given way to vocal music that is decorative and melismatic, while instrumental performance hints at language patterns through its modal ornamentations. Song plays a principal role in Vietnamese culture, and everyone is encouraged to sing. Instrumental music is usually reserved for professionally trained musicians, to be performed on special rather than daily occasions.

General Characteristics

Children's songs, folk songs, and theater and instrumental music derived from a sophisticated system of pitch and rhythmic components are all part of Vietnamese musical expression. Rhythm and melody are based on the principle called *hoa lá*, or "adding flowers and leaves." This means a realization of variation and improvisation from a schematic structure – a skeleton that may be fleshed out with various embellishments by the performer. Some genres of Vietnamese music date back to a thousand years ago. Traditional songs, instrumental music for entertainment, theater forms, ritual music, Buddhist chant, and water puppet plays and dance forms are a part of the oldest layer of Vietnamese music. Songs sung during or after work in the ricefields, mountains, rivers and seacoasts contain texts which reflect the natural surroundings of farmers and fishermen that have remained unchanged through the centuries.

In earlier times, the elite classes of Vietnamese people, including the rulers, scholars and nobility, expected music and dance to adhere to clearly-defined practices, theoretical concepts, formal classification of instruments, and theatrical codifications. Because the great majority of Vietnamese citizens have worked as farmers, however, the music has come to bear certain "folk" characteristics. Vietnamese folk music has influenced art styles, and art music has had a clear impact on folk genres. While folk song is closely linked to agricultural life, expressing local customs and occupational skills, art music includes an elaborate system of modes and requires high performance skills. Today, the most appropriate description of Vietnamese music is the term "traditional," which implies the convergence of art music with folk characteristics.

Genres of Music

There are numerous genres and sub-genres of music. They have appeared in the stream of historical and geographical development, and relate to particular social stratifications. The best known are:

Common Musical Genres	
Dân Ca	Folk Songs
Hát Ả Đào	Northern Chamber Music
Ca Huế	Central Chamber Music
Nhạc Tài Tử	Southern Chamber Music
Hát Chèo	Northern Folk Theater
Hát Bội	Classical Theater
Hát Cải Lương	Southern Reformed Theater
Lễ Nhạc Phật Giáo	Buddhist Liturgy
Tân Nhạc	Modernized vocal music
	(see below)

Since the middle of the twentieth century, the modernized kind of vocal music called *tân nhạc* has been performed in urban areas with strong European influence. Musical instruments and theory are borrowed from Western traditions, while the sung language remains Vietnamese. In general, the natural quality of the voice is preferred for folk songs. Certain characters of the classical theater (*hát bội*) sing in a falsetto voice that is carefully studied and practiced for many years.

Vietnamese music may be *monophonic* (having a single line of melody without harmony or other accompanying melodies, even if accompanied simply as long as the melody is self-sufficient) or *heterophonic* (a melody performed simultaneously by more than one individual, each adding their own modifications). In fact, a single piece may intersperse examples of both types of texture. A melody may be sung or played as a delicate solo that requires the listener's careful attention so that subtly-ornamented pitches can be fully appreciated, unlike the experience derived from music employing "block-chord progressions." Instrumental music is usually heterophonic, while songs are more frequently sung in monophonic style. Percussion instruments, led by drums, are frequently played together to create a *polyrhythm* (rhythm patterns that are superimposed on each other). Stringed instruments may also be played either with a basic melody or in a more developed way that includes improvisational variations. Understandably, it is not easy for a new listener to distinguish a basic melody from a developed melody of a piece until familiarity with the melody and style is established. In some pieces, the melodic texture can become quite complex as several instruments are played together at one time.

Melody

The *dynamics* depend upon the genre, the ensemble and the character of the individual piece. Chamber music is performed at a moderate level of dynamics, due to the predominance of stringed instruments in most ensembles and also because small audiences usually prevail at these performances. Theatrical and ritual music performances are likely to be of greater intensity, due partly to the use of percussion instruments in these orchestras and perhaps also to larger crowds.

Dynamics

The *rhythm* of Vietnamese music is most often set within the frame of duple meter; performers often improvise over a basic cyclical structure of 2, 4 or 8 beats. Children's songs, song games, and folk dances are metrically fixed, while instrumental music often proceeds from a free and improvisatory section to regular temporal measurement at a later time. Traditional instrumental music often begins slowly and increases in speed to the end.

Rhythm

Tonally, Vietnamese traditional music is based on one of a variety of scales that range from two to seven pitches. Many of the scales bear traces of a particular region. Once having listened to pitches and intervals, it is often possible to identify the origin of a song. At the very least, a trained listener will know the music as "Northern," "Central" or "Southern." The ornamentation or intonational patterns of Vietnamese music can be quite intricate. Certain ornaments are associated with scale

Tonality

degrees or particular songs.   The pentatonic scale is the most prevalent, with its five pitches comprising such scales as these:

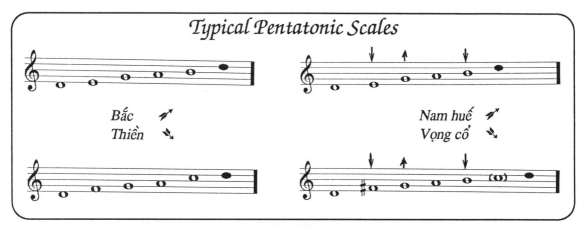

Đàn tam thập lục, hammered dulcimer, played by Ms. Doan Trang Dieu Nguyen.

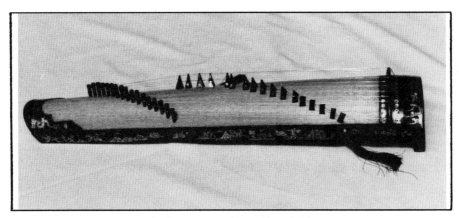

A *đàn tranh,* seventeen-stringed zither.

Phong Nguyen playing the *đàn tranh* zither (left), *đàn nguyệt* lute, (right), and *đàn bầu or đàn độc huyền* monochord,(below).
Bottom Right: Phong Nguyen introducing children to the *đàn bầu* during a visit to an elementary school.

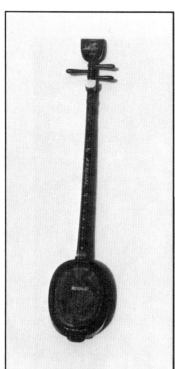
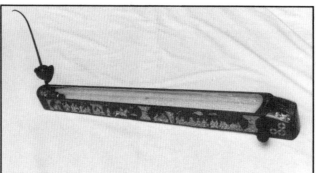
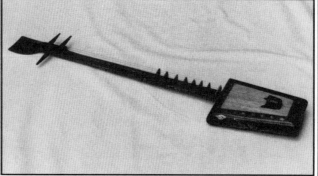

(above) Đàn tam, a three-stringed fretless lute.

(top) Đàn bầu or *đàn độc huyền*, a monochord.
(above) Đàn đáy, a trapezoidal back-less lute.

(above) Đàn nguyệt, a long-necked moon-shaped lute.

A young student of the *đàn tranh* zither. (above)
Đàn đoản, a short-necked, moon-shaped lute. (below)

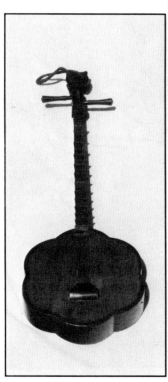
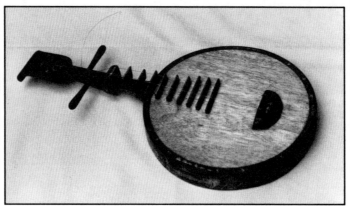

Đàn xến, an octagonal lute.

Đàn tỳ bà, a pear-shaped lute.

Vietnamese Musical Instruments

The aesthetic of the music concerns itself with timbre as well as pitch, and some music may require performance on specific instruments. While vocal types are important, the numerous instruments and their genres are also quite intriguing to students of Vietnamese music. The two major groups of instruments are *strings* and *percussion*. Wind instruments, although fewer, add an interesting timbre to the others.

Stringed instruments include plucked lutes, zithers, bowed fiddles and hammered dulcimers. The strings themselves are commonly made of silk or *Strings* metal. Wood and coconut shells are used to make the body of fiddles, lutes and zithers. The pegs and decorative trimmings may consist of ivory, bamboo, buffalo horn, shell, animal bone or skin, and horsetail hair. Most of these instruments are inlaid with mother-of-pearl, a sign of the proximity of much of Vietnam to the sea.

> *Important Vietnamese Stringed Instruments (see photos)*
> đàn bầu — a monochord (one-stringed) zither
> đàn nguyệt — a moon-shaped two-stringed plucked lute
> đàn tranh — a 16- or 17-stringed zither resembling the
> Chinese zheng or Japanese koto
> đàn nhị — a two-stringed fiddle
> đàn gáo — a two-stringed coconut shell fiddle
> đàn tam thập lục — a hammered dulcimer

The *đàn nhị* a, a two-stringed fiddle, played by Mr. Tam Tri (Le Van Thanh).

A *đàn gáo*, a two-stringed coconut shell fiddle.

Percussion instruments include drums, gongs, cymbals, xylo-
phones, wooden clappers, wooden or bamboo "bells," and bronze bells.
They function as solo instruments, as accompaniment to vocal music, or in
ensemble arrangements. Materials such as wood, cow or buffalo skins, bamboo, stone and
bronze offer various tones and tone colors.

Common Percussion Instruments

trống	drum
mõ	wooden or bamboo bell
t'rưng	bamboo xylophone
chập chõa	pair of cymbals
chiêng	gong
sinh tiền	coin clapper
song lang	foot clapper (*see photo*)

Drum dance.

A very old *đại cơ* (big temple drum) presented by the Nguyen dynasty
of Vietnam to the French government in Paris in the 1880s.

Song lang, foot clapper.

Wind instruments include the bamboo flute, which can be blown vertically or transversely. Flutes have holes, rather than keys, that are open, covered, or partially covered by the fingers. Double-reed oboes and conch shells are used in performance by lowland people, and mouth organs by the highland minority people called *thượng*.

Common Wind Instruments

sáo	transverse flute
tiêu	vertical flute
kèn	double-reed oboe
m'buat	mouth organ
hải loa	conch shell

Nghia Dinh Nguyen playing the *sáo*. Bamboo flutes are made in several sizes.

Vietnamese music is tremendously varied, and the listener is unlikely to find it uniform. From piece to piece, and from performance to performance, the characteristics of spontaneity, variation, improvisation, and collective composition abound. The companion tape to this volume offers ample opportunities to become immersed in the sound of traditional Vietnamese vocal and instrumental music and recited poetry. Theoretical details of the music are found written in scholarly sources, but a true understanding of the deep emotions of love, joy and sorrow expressed through this music will arise from exposure to the music itself, through listening and performance.

Vietnamese Music in the United States

In 1989, there were 800,000 Vietnamese immigrants living in the United States. This immigrant population, formerly called "refugees," is now well-integrated into American society. Most have become American citizens or are in the process of becoming naturalized. Among these is found a significant number of musicians, singers, actors and actresses who embody a distinctive musical culture in California, Texas, Washington, Massachusetts, Connecticut, New York, Illinois, Ohio, Minnesota, and in several other communities throughout the United States.

Common Musical Genres in the United States

dân ca	folk song
nhạc tài tử	chamber music, reserved largely for connoisseurs of music
ritual music	of the Buddhist liturgy
cải lương	reformed theater, performed for large audiences of several thousand people
châù văn	music for sacred text singing and dancing in shamanist temples
tân nhạc	"modern" Westernized music

These six genres are showing great vitality throughout the United States. *Dân ca,* originally peasants' folksongs, thrive in many urban communal events. They are short occupational or entertainment songs that are easily accessible because of their vernacular language and sweet and simple melodies. Lullabies, boat songs, antiphonal boy-girl songs, and metaphorical songs are particularly popular sub-types of the *dân ca.*

The instrumental and vocal entertainment music called *nhạc tài tử* survives among selected immigrant groups in their private homes. The *đàn tranh* zither, *đàn bầu* monochord, and *đàn nguyệt* lute are featured in this art music genre. *Nhạc tài tử* is organized within a modal framework. Traditional melodies are maintained as the core of a piece, but improvisation within the principles of the mode allows for a highly expressive and personalized music.

The chanting of Buddhist sutra is commonly practiced in about sixty Vietnamese temples from the east to west coasts of the United States. Buddhist priests and monks are often supported and sheltered by a particular community, in a house which serves as a temple for all except the larger celebrations or rituals. In ceremonies requiring amounts of food and flowers, all pitch in to provide the necessities. A Buddhist liturgical ceremony, such as the Anniversary of Buddha's Birthday may attract thousands of participants. On this occasion, music festivals are often organized in the temple yard or in a public auditorium (perhaps in a school or lodge) nearby. Chanted texts in romanized characters have been reprinted in fairly extensive quantities for services. Because Buddhism has had a 2,000-year history in Vietnam, it serves as a cultural shelter for many immigrants.

While there are several classical and folk theater forms in Vietnam, only the *cải lương* of southern Vietnam is performed in the United States. *Cải lương* is extremely popular, and has fashioned its plots from Vietnamese legends, history, contemporary politics, and religious beliefs. Instrumental music, singing and dancing are key to the theatrical performance, and contemporary staging includes scenery, lighting, and amplification through state-of-the-art sound systems. Much of the music of *cải lương* derives from the *nhạc tài tử* (see previous page) which was the original inspiration for the theater form in 1919-1920. The favorite song of Vietnamese immigrants, "*Vọng Cổ*" (Longing for the Past) is usually included in the *cải lương*. To many Vietnamese, "*Vọng Cổ*" is *cải lương* —and vice versa. New plays are currently being written and produced, audio and video tapes are available for purchase, and the training of actors and actresses continues in many Vietnamese immigrant communities.

Hát bội classical theater performance, dramatizing the story of the Sisters Trung.

Chầu văn, shamanist chanting and dancing, are infrequently found in several West Coast temples, and in Texas. *Chầu văn* is oriented toward the achievement of trance-like states, and is accompanied by live or recorded music. The practice originated in certain tribal rituals of the Hmong and Tai mountain people.

The Westernized music called *tân nhạc* originated during the French colonial period. *Tân nhạc* uses Western instrumentation and Vietnamese lyrics, and often utilizes Vietnamese folk melodies as well. Once an easy-listening music, it is now the rage for young people in its adaptation as "new wave" Vietnamese rock. Vietnamese songs as well as translated versions of American, French, Chinese and Japanese songs are available on audio and video cassette tapes.

The music of pre-1975 Vietnam continues to be performed, and forms the basis for new compositions in Vietnamese communities in the United States. Life in exile and love of the native land are recurrent song themes, as are new songs dealing with social, political, revolutionary (anti-communist), and educational matters. While the new social context may eventually impact upon the course of Vietnamese traditional music in the U.S., Vietnamese-Americans hold great regard for the songs and instrumental music of their mother country in the first fifteen years of their exile.[1]

---

1. For a more comprehensive examination of the forms of music in the principal Vietnamese communities in the United States see Music in Exile: Music of the Vietnamese Immigrants in the United States by Phong Nguyen (see bibliography).

Vietnamese performing artists in the United States. From left to right:
Tam Tri, Thu Van, Phong Nguyen (author), Kim Tuyen, Kim Oanh and Hoang Oanh.

3 *"Who brought the blackbird to the other side of the river?"*
A Guide to the Music of Vietnam

The lessons which follow are designed for use by groups with the guidance of a teacher or by individuals working independently with the tape and book. They may be used equally effectively within a music curriculum or in other disciplines, and by Vietnamese as well as non-Vietnamese readers. This set introduces clearly, concisely yet comprehensively varied aspects of Vietnamese music, geography, language and literature, folklore, customs and culture. The lessons are experience-oriented, and will help to develop listening skills, rhythmic responses, the singing voice, and critical thinking about Vietnamese music, the related arts, and their context within the culture. The cultural treasures of Vietnam are awaiting discovery in these experiences with folk songs, instrumental pieces and stories.

Using the Lessons

The lessons provide a logical sequence for teaching and learning. Each corresponds to a recorded selection, found in the same order on the companion tape. Songs are notated, and each is presented with its text, pronunciation, and translation. Background information included sets each piece in its cultural context. Thus the music is not a collection of abstract and unrelated sound artifacts, but reflections of the environment and the traditional ceremonies, thoughts, feelings, beliefs, and daily living patterns of the Vietnamese.

We offer step-by-step procedures, to enable the user to clearly see the nature of a lesson directed toward developing musical skills and cultural understanding. Use the lessons as a starting point, and tailor them to suit classroom or community or personal needs. Each may be presented as a self-contained unit, expanded or shortened as needed. We have suggested age and grade levels, but these are flexible and may be adjusted when there is a specific agenda in mind for a given lesson. You will also find ideas for generating discussion, and for further musical experiences that include listening, singing, movement and instrumental performance.

Vietnamese performance style is quite delicate—soft and rather transparent. The singing of students of this music should be reflective of this style. "Street voices" are left behind; rather the light "head voice" is far more characteristic in performance. *Listening is central to the experiences these lessons provide.* Careful and concentrated listening will reveal the nuances of the language, vocal techniques and instrumental performance that are impossible to write down accurately. Because the music is likely to be unfamiliar to American users of the set, preliminary and then repeated listening will be critical to appreciation and understanding. Warm-up exercises are recommended to ease the way for the eventual singing of songs that are based on these uncommon scales, modes and tunings. Vocal exercises along these lines and frequent exposure to the companion tape will better prepare students for performing in a manner characteristic of the style.

Performance Style

Those who are using this set with a class are well advised to listen to the tape far in advance of a class presentation. Play the tape in the car, at meals, while conducting routine tasks—the greater the familiarity with the songs, the greater the ease and enthusiasm for the music. Guided listening as well as informal "sound baths" serve to acquaint newcomers to the style. Aural immersion gradually leads to the ability to sing with and respond rhythmically to the music. The result of this refreshing *ear opening* experience is not only an enjoyment of the music but also sensitive insight into the Vietnamese people and their culture and perhaps even the willingness to listen to other musics of the world with increased openness and perception.

Finally, there are many ways to enhance the overall learning experience: by showing photographs of Vietnam and Vietnamese people, *Follow-Up* telling Vietnamese folk tales, playing films and videotapes on historical and contemporary Vietnam, eating Vietnamese food, and listening informally to other recordings during unrelated activities. Invite Vietnamese residents of your community to visit your group, and encourage discussions and interviews with them or others who have lived or travelled anywhere in Vietnam or elsewhere in Southeast Asia. Check the bibliography for written or recorded resources for further involvement.

Vietnamese children playing in the United States.

I. Hát Đúm

"Now everybody feels relaxed after work"

"I learned this from a North Vietnamese woman, a refugee living in Saigon when I lived there. Those who are born in north, central or southern parts of Vietnam do not have contact with people of other regions, because of transportation difficulties, so the southerners seldom know northern songs. Folk songs like this are sung in the villages, in the countryside. This one is quite interesting and rare because it only uses two tones. Vietnamese language has six tones. The actual structure of the piece uses only the two tones, but the gliding tones are necessary for people to understand the words."

During several days of village festivals in North Vietnam, groups of boys and girls meet in the temple's yard and sing songs, one after another, expressing love, the joys of meeting, or wishes for better friendship. *"Hát Đúm"* is found among these antiphonal folk song styles. *"Hát"* means "singing" and *"đúm"* is a "crowd" or "group"; thus, the translation is "singing in (or by) a group." Most of these songs are made from folk poems with couplets of six and eight syllables, or seven-, seven-, six- and eight-syllable verses.

The recording features a girls' version of *"Hát Đúm,"* originating from Hai Duong Province. The song generally precedes a game of any sort, serving as an introduction, or preparation for players who might take part in games, jokes and song contests that may follow. The song has only two tones at the interval of a fifth, making it an appropriate introduction to Vietnamese language and melody for any age.

Ngày hôm nay thanh nhàn thong thả
(Ngie home nah-ee thahn nyang thawng thah)
Chị em ta còn lạ chưa quen
(Tsi aim tah corn lah tsew-ah kwen)

Không chơi thì bảo rằng hèn
(Kowng tser-ee thee bao zahng hair-en)
Chơi ra chúng bạn chê khen thế nào
(Tser-ee zah tsoo-ng barn tsay koenthay nah- or)

Translation:

Now everybody feels relaxed after their work.
We are not yet well-acquainted, but games should be fun to play together.
If I don't join the games, I may be thought of as unskilled.
I don't want my friends to judge me.

Words and Pronunciation:

Ngày hôm nay thanh nhàn thong thả
(Ngie home nah-ee thahn nyang thawng thah)
Chị em ta còn lạ chưa quen
(Tsi aim tah korn lah tsew-ah kwen)
Không chơi thì bảo rằng hèn
(Kowng tser-ee thee bao zaang hair-en)
Chơi ra chúng bạn chê khen thế nào
(Tser-ee zah tsoo-ng barn tsay kaen thay nah-or)

Teaching/Learning Sequence   **Level: early childhood, K-2**

1. **Describe the circumstances of the song using the following questions as a guide:**
    *   *What does "hát đúm" mean?* (Singing in or by a group.)
    *   *Where is this song style found?* (In Hai Duong Province, between Hanoi and the Gulf of Tonkin.)
    *   *Where is the song usually sung?* (In the yard of a Buddhist temple.)
    *   *What is the occasion and purpose of the song?* (As a preparation for games that follow.)

2. **Listen to the recording:**
    *   *How many pitches does the melody contain?* (2)
    *   *Tap the repeated ostinato-like rhythm:* ♩ ♩

3. **Prepare to sing the song:**
    *   *Sing exercise #1 .* The teacher presents each two-measure phrase, then the students imitate. Once these patterns are familiar, eliminate the echoing and sing the short melodic phrases together once, twice, or three times; try different tempi.

Do Sol Sol Sol Re La La La Mi Ti Ti Ti Fa Do

Do Do Sol Re Re Re La Mi Mi Mi La Mi La

Exercise 1

*   *Pronounce each phrase in its melodic rhythm,* while conducting the pulse.
    How many syllables are there in each phrase? (7,7,6,8)
    This is the characteristic form of *hát đúm* songs.

4. **Sing the song:**
    *   Sing "la" or the words while tapping the melodic rhythm.
    *   Sing while patting the lap (*patsch*) on each low pitch and clapping each high pitch.
    *   Sing antiphonally in two groups. Group I sings phrases 1 and 3, Group II sings phrases 2 and 4. Reverse roles.
    *   Sing antiphonally, but this time step the melodic rhythm when singing, and remain still when not singing.

II. Cùm Nụm Cùm Nịu

"Close your hands!"

I learned this game song by ear from my friends when I was five or six, living in Tam Ngai in the Mekong Delta. I remember playing it in the front yard of my house, or in the temple yard. The words in this song are not related to each other except by sound - they were put together because of the sound of the rhyme, not because of any particular meaning. (The rhyme at the end of each line rhymes with another word in the middle of the next phrase.) They serve to distract everybody, to confuse the fists!

As in the West, children in Vietnam play a game of hide-and-seek. In choosing a person to be "it" to seek the others, they sing a counting-out rhyme. All of the participating children close their hands into a fist, and put one fist on top of another in a long and high vertical column. One child counts the hands by touching them with an index finger, first up and then down the column of fists, touching one fist for each pulse. On the last word/beat, the owner of the last fist touched is "it." The seeker covers his/her eyes and counts to ten while the other children run to hiding places. This particular counting-out rhyme is played by children in South Vietnam.

The song contains only four pitches. While you are listening note that the "en" and "an" endings are prolonged and sound like "en-ng" and "an-ng." The "ch" sound is softer and lighter than in a North Vietnamese song like *"Hát Đúm."*

Translation:

Close your hands! Close your hands! Pretty hands, fairy's hands.
Golden coins, chop-stick. A grain of rice making three flowers.
The thief steals eggs. Beetles and insects.
Snakes and centipedes. It's this hand!

Words and Pronunciation:

Cùm nụm cùm nịu, tay tí, tay tiên

> *(koom noom koom new, tah-ee tee tah-ee tee-en)*

Đồng tiền chiếc đũa, hột lúa ba bông

> *(dong tee-en tsee-ek doo-ah, hoh(t) loo-ah bah boh-ng)*

Ăn trộm ăn cắp, trứng gà

> *(ahng troh-m ahng kahp, trew-ng gah)*

Bù xa bù xích

> *(boo sah boo sik)*

Con rắn con rít, thì ra tay nầy.

> *(korn rahng korn reet, thee rah tah-ee nay-ee)*

Teaching/Learning Sequence   **Level: early childhood, K-4**

1. **Describe the function of the song.** (It is a counting-out rhyme.)
   Find or recall counting-out rhymes common in the United States, such as those offered below. Encourage students to demonstrate others from their own cultural backgrounds.

   "One potato, two potato, three potato, four
   Five potato, six potato, seven potato, more."

   "Engine, engine, number nine,
   Going down Chicago Line,
   If the train should jump the track,
   Do you want your money back? [Child answers "yes" or "no"]
   Y-E-S spells yes, and you are not it."

2. **Listen to the recording:**
   - *Does this song have a steady pulse?* (Yes; most counting-out rhymes do.)
   - *What is the meter of the song?* (Duple.)
   - *Keep the duple meter* by tapping closed fists on the lap (beat 1) and clapping (beat 2).

3. **Prepare to sing the song:**
   - *Sing exercise #2.* The teacher sings suggested tonal patterns, followed by student imitation. Teacher and students may improvise other patterns that utilize two, three and four pitches of the song, with or without solfege syllables.
   - ~Review the pitch components of the song by singing suggested tonal patterns, then challenge students to sing the entire song with solfege syllables and hand signals, if appropriate, slowly at first and then with increasing speed.

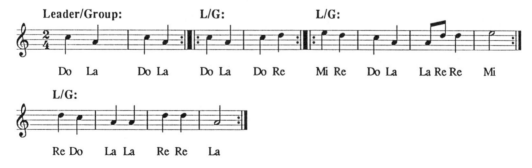

Exercise 2

4. **Sing the song:**
   - Sing together while keeping the duple meter as in (2) above or by pounding the left closed fist with the right and vice versa.
   - Divide the group into units of four or five participants, and choose one person in each group to count stacked fists while the others sing the song.
   - Emphasize the pulse with a muted drum beat while the group sings and pounds their own fists or steps the rhythm.

III. Xây Khăn
"I am shaking the handkerchief up and down"

I learned this also when I was five or six. We played it as a kind of trial or test of our sensitivity—we believed that even if you do not see you have to feel, to sense. If the child in front of the handkerchief did not realize the handkerchief was behind him, the child who was "it" would grab the cloth and pretend to "beat" him with it. The others would laugh and tease him. Even so, the child who had been singled out would become the next "it."

      This is a game song popular with Vietnamese children that tests their awareness and concentration. Participants sit cross-legged in a circle on the floor. One child is selected to hold a handkerchief and walk around the circle, behind the participants. As the group sings *"Xây Khăn,"* the child drops the handkerchief secretly behind one of the other children. As the song finishes, the child behind whom the handkerchief is lying must be aware that it has been dropped there. He identifies himself, and then takes his turn as the game starts again. If he does not, he is teased by the others! The presence of the water buffalo in the words indicates this is a game of the countryside. Even though it is an extremely common animal in the country, so many Vietnamese are living their entire lives in urban surroundings that many have never seen and do not know what a water buffalo is.

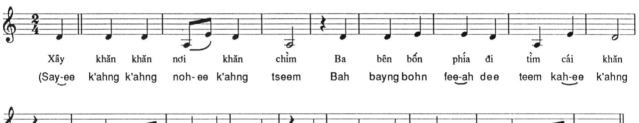

Translation:

I am shaking the handkerchief which is flowing up and down.
People on three sides and four corners will go find it.
Hey! Look over there:
the water buffalo keeper is wearing a torn shirt that shows his shoulder!
Nobody patches it for him, so he must wear it forever.

Words and Pronunciation:

Xây khăn khăn nổi khăn chìm

    (Say-ee k'ahng k'ahng noh-ee k'ahng tseem)

Ba bên bốn phía đi tìm cái khăn

    (Bah bayng boh-n fee-ah dee teem kah-ee k'ahng)

Thằng chăn bận áo rách vai

    (thahng tsahng bahng ao rah-ak yah-ee)

Không ai may vá thằng chăn bận hoài

    (K'oh-ng ah-ee mah-ee ya thahng tsahng bahng hwa-ee)

Teaching/Learning Sequence   Level: early childhood, K-3

1. **Describe the nature of the game song.**
   - *Does the game appear similar in any way to other game songs students may know?* Circle games are commonly played by children in many cultures, and are often associated with a particular song. Examples of circle game songs include "Bluebird," "Little Sally Walker," "Little Johnny Brown" (which also uses a handkerchief), "Looby Loo," "Hokey Pokey," "*Kagome*" from Japan, and "*Oboo Asi Me Nsa*" from Ghana. Choose some of these circle game songs and compare their functions and the "object of the game."

2. **Listen to the recording:**
   - *How many phrases are there?* (4)
     ~Show the phrases by drawing curved lines in space [⌒⌒⌒⌒]
   - *Tap the pulse. Are there any rhythms that are faster than the pulse?* (Yes, ♩♩)
     ~*Are there any that are slower?* (Yes, ♩)

3. **Prepare to sing the song:**
   - While tapping the pulse, pronounce each phrase in rhythm.

4. **Sing the song:**
   - Sing the song together while tapping the rhythm of the melody, including all ♫ and ♩
   - Sing together and step the rhythm of the melody.
   - Play the game, encouraging children to continue singing so that the child with the handkerchief can step rhythmically around the circle.

Water buffalo threshing rice near Cam Ranh.

IV. Cò Lả

"The egret is flying, flying"

I learned this while taking part in various activities in high school and college in Saigon. Many people in Saigon know this song even though it is a very typical, popular song and melody of North Vietnam, particularly in the area of the northern delta of the Red River. It was played on the radio throughout Vietnam when I was a teenager. After I learned it I later taught it to my own class.

"*Cò Lả*" is one of the most beautiful folk songs of North Vietnam. It is sung by peasants in rural areas and by professionals in stage performances in the cities, although the words vary. There are also numerous versions of the melody. Variants are due to language intonations of the six- and eight-syllable verses, a standard rule of Vietnamese poetry. However the melodic pattern of the *cò lả* style within the refrain remains the same.

The egret, the bird sung about in this song, is a type of heron with a long neck and spearlike legs. A large wading bird, it enjoys marshes and coastal tidal flats and is found in Vietnam as well as in Florida and the coastal states of the United States. In this song, the egret symbolizes a friend or loved one who has gone away, and the singer asks of him or her, "Do you remember me?"

In Vietnam, the refrain is sung by a group of people, while the lead singer must be skillful in poetic and melodic improvisation within fixed rhythm patterns. The dialect is North Vietnamese. The recording features accompaniment by the *đàn bầu* , a Vietnamese monochord, and the *đàn tranh,* a metal string zither. (*see photos*) These instruments play the introduction, interludes, and also accompany the singers, occasionally using minor variations of the melody to enrich and embellish the vocal line while it is being sung.

Translation:

1. The egret is flying, flying, flying from the City Hall
Back to Dong Dang. (*The name of a village.*)

    Refrain: Ting ting tang, tang ting ting
        Oh, my beloved, my beloved
        Do you remember me? Do you miss me?

2. Dong Dang has the Ky Lua street area (*Where specialized goods are sold.*)
There is Miss To Thi, there is the temple Tam Thanh.

3. Somebody is going to Lang province (*"Somebody" in this case is an indirect address of the particular person "you," which would not be a delicate enough form of address for the beloved.*)
Please remember, tell people I always feel grateful to your parents, who gave birth and raised you.

Words and Pronunciation:

1. Con cò cò bay lã lã bay la, Bay qua qua cửa phủ
   (korn kaw kaw bay-ee lah lah bay-ee lah, bay-ee kwa kwa kew-ah foo)
   Bay về về Đồng Đăng
   (Bay-ee vay vay dong dahng)

   Refrain: Tỉnh tỉnh tang, tang tỉng tỉnh
   (Ting ting tahng, tahng ting ting)
   Duyên tỉnh rằng, duyên tỉnh ơi
   (Ziyen ting zahng ziyen ting er-ee)
   Rằng có biết là biết hay chăng (2x)
   (Zahng kor bee-eht lah bee-eht hay-ee tsahng)

2. Đồng Đăng (Đăng) có phố (phố) Kỳ Lừa
   (Dohng Dahng (Dahng) kor foh (foh) Kee Lew-ah)
   Có nàng (nàng) Tô Thị, có chùa (chùa) Tam Thanh
   (kor nahng (nahng) Toh Thee, kor tsoo-ah (tsoo-ah) Tahm Thahnh)

3. Ai lên (lên) xứ Lạng (Lạng) cùng anh
   (ah-ee layne (layne) seeyoo Lahng (Lahng) koo-ng ahnh)
   Tiếc công (công) bác mẹ, sinh thành (thành) ra em
   (Tee-ehk kohng (kohng) bark mae, sing thahng (thahnh) za aem)

Paddling a typical riverboat in South Vietnam.

Cò Lả

Teaching/Learning Sequence   Level: Grade 2 - adult

(The song may be transposed to suit the group's comfortable voice range.)

1. Discuss:

- *Discuss the matter of fixed and improvised music,* and the importance of variation and personal interpretation in folk and traditional music of Vietnam and other parts of the world.
- *Discuss the poetic text,* including the symbolism of the flying bird. (The Puerto Rican song *"La Paloma se Fué"* also uses the image of a bird that has flown away, never to return. The Appalachian song "The Cuckoo" has a similar feeling.)

2. Listen to the recording:

- *What is the organization of the song? Are there different sections?* (Yes, solo and refrain.)

  ~*What American folk songs are organized in a similar way?* ("Oh, Susanna," "Old Joe Clark" and others). Sing them.
- *Conduct the meter during the solo section,* and clap (with two fingers) and snap for the refrain. What is the meter? (Duple)
- *Note the slight tremolo* in the voice and monochord (indicated in the score by ~).
- *Name and describe* the type of instruments that accompany the singers. (*Đàn tranh* and *đàn bầu*; stringed, plucked zithers.)
- *Do these instruments play together with the voice?* (With the singers and also as introduction and for interludes.)

3. Prepare to sing the song:

- *Pronounce each phrase in its melodic rhythm,* continuing to clap and snap the meter pulses.

4. Sing the song:

- *Sing the refrain* together.
- *Sing exercise #3,* noting the difference between a plain and an ornamented melody. Sing with solfege and/or neutral syllables (la, ah etc.).

Exercise 3

- Sing the song together. Conduct and stand still for the solo. Walk the pulse, clap and snap the meter pulses, and sing the refrain.

V. Lý Chim Quyên

"Song of the Nightingale"

My family, although musicians, have long been farmers of rice and also fruit trees— orange, tangerine, banana, mango and others. Our fruit orchard stretched over several acres. Sometimes in the afternoon people of all ages would get together in the yard of our brick house and sing. When I was very young my mother sometimes sang this to me while she did needlework. I remember thinking that she and my father must have learned the lesson in the song, because they never divorced and had a solid marriage and strong family.

The reference to the fighting fish is an interesting one. Usually these beautifully colored fish live in a pond, river or lake. We used to catch them, and raise them in glass containers — one to a bowl. If they were placed together in one, they would fight like mortal enemies, even to death. After school, we would place the bowls near each other with a sheet of paper between the bowls so the fish could not see each other and get agitated. Then we would put different ones together, and watch the fighting to see which was the best. If the fight became too violent, we might separate them so they would not kill each other. They would calm down quickly when placed again in their own glass pot.

"*Lý Chim Quyên*" is a folk song sung by farmers during their leisure time. This song of comparison (see the text) originates from popular verse, which stressses the importance of love through familiarity and understanding, rather than the idea of romantically falling into love or love at first sight, common themes in American songs. The nightingale is a prominent bird featured in Vietnamese literature, from folk tales to classical poetry. Its song is rumored to be among the most beautiful of birdsongs in the world. The poem compares the familiarity of the nightingale with its favorite yellow berry, with the deep-rooted familiarity between a husband and wife. The suggestion (and the honored value inherent) is that we feel comfortable with people, places, and objects that we know and understand, and find fundamental sustenance and security in these people and things. Even the fierce fighting fish returns to the safe haven of its holding tank when the battle is over.

The rhymed words at the sixth syllable of a pair of six-and eight-syllable phrases are characteristic of certain Vietnamese poems:

Chim quyên ăn trái nhãn lòng
1   2   3 4 5 **6***

Lia thia quen chậu vợ chồng quen hơi
1   2   3   4   5 **6*** 7   8

The scale used is specific to the Southern region of Vietnam.

The *dàn tranh* zither is used to accompany the song. Its sixteen strings are tuned as follows:

This is a non-tempered scale. The pitches B⁻ and E⁻ are tuned about 30 Ellis cents lower than B and E. To obtain the pitch E⁻ as heard on the recording, the *dàn tranh* player pushes on the D string and quickly bends it to E⁻. Such a bending offers a graceful flavor to the song. The strings of the *dàn tranh* are plucked with finger nails or metal picks worn on the thumb (T), index (I) and middle (M) fingers of the right hand.

Translation:

The nightingale eats the yellow berries.
> Oh, my dear friend. Oh, my dear friend.

The fighting fish knows its pot.
The husband and wife know each other's scent.
> Oh, my dear friend.

Words and pronunciation

Soloist: Chim quyên quầy, ăn trái quây,
> (Tseem weeng way-ee, ahng try-ee way-ee)
nhãn nhãn lòng, nhãn nhãn lòng
> (nyang nyang lohng, nyang nyang lohng)

Chorus, Refrain: Ớ con bạn mình ơi. Ớ con bạn mình ơi.
> (er korn bahng ming oy, er korn bahng ming oy)

Soloist: Lia thia quầy , Quen chậu quây
> (lee-ya thee-ya way-ee, weng tser-oo way-ee)
Vợ vợ chồng Vợ vợ chồng
> (Yah-er ah-yer tsohng-ah, yah-er ah-yer tsohng)

Chorus, Refrain: Ớ con bạn quen hơi. Ớ con bạn mình hơi.
> (er korn bahng weng oy, er korn bahng weng oy)

Lý Chim Quyên

(Lee tseem kwu-eeng)

↑ = sounds slightly higher; ↓ = sounds slightly lower

Teaching/Learning Sequence　　　　　　**Level: Grade 4 to Adult**

1.　Describe the text, its meaning and its rhyming scheme.
　　　How do the ideas expressed in the poem relate to our own lives? You might consider things that are familiar and therefore liked or seen in a positive light, and the possibility that we might be somewhat suspicious of things we do not know well. How does this relate to our taste in music? Our feelings about people? If the group includes teenage or adult members, discuss courtship and marriage in various cultures, the idea of romantic love and "love at first sight" in contrast to the custom of arranged marriages.

2.　Listen to the recording:
- *Conduct the meter.*
- *What is the meter of the song?* (Duple.)
- *What is the form or structure of the song?* (Solo and refrain; two verses and refrain repeat twice)
    - ~ What other songs have a similar structure? (*"Cò Lả," "Old Joe Clark," "Oh Susanna"*)
- *Describe the accompaniment.* (The *đàn tranh* zither is playing a slightly different melody from the voice—a simultaneous variation.)
    - ~ *Describe* the manner of playing and tuning the *đàn tranh.*
    - ~ *Demonstrate the voice and đàn tranh relationship* by singing while playing the zither part on the piano or another instrument. This is an example of heterophonic texture, common to many Vietnamese instrumental pieces.

3.　Play and sing the *G natural minor scale* (below). Note that the tuning of this piece is not quite "minor", but leaning in that direction:

G Natural Minor Scale

4.　Prepare to sing the song:
- *Sing exercise #4.* The scale and patterns will reinforce the song's mode.

Exercise 4

- While keeping or conducting the pulse, pronounce the phrases in rhythm.

5.　Sing the song:
- *Sing the refrain* of the song together listening carefully to the *đàn tranh* accompaniment during the solo sections.

VI. Qua Cầu Gió Bay

"The Wind on the Bridge"

People all over Saigon sang this song, and I heard it in about 1966 when I lived there. It was such a lovely song that I learned it, then later taught it to my students. I also enjoy the sentiment expressed by the words, that when we are in love, we do not any longer care what our parents think...we can be "liars" when we love, to cover up for the generous gestures we make to the loved one. In this case, the singer has given away his shirt, his pyramid or cone-shaped hat, and a ring to his beloved. It all has to be kept a secret, because the parents might say it is too direct, or not proper to give these things as gifts. Parents will say that we have to obey rules and propriety, but when in love we don't care!

Ha Bac province is the cradle of Vietnamese culture. The first capital city of Vietnam was located there in the first century. Many poems were written by dignitaries of the court, and the words were very polished and refined. Some found their way into quan họ songs.

"Qua Cầu Gió Bay" is one of the best known of a genre of songs that involve antiphonal group singing. Called *hát quan họ* or *quan họ* of Ha Bac (formerly Bac Ninh) Province near Hanoi, this is one of the most important and respected folk traditions in Vietnam. *Quan họ* singing typically takes place during spring and autumn festivals centered around the agrarian themes of planting and harvesting. During these festivals groups of young people gather in a house, on a hill, by a lake, in a rice field, or in the Buddhist temple yard. Over the course of several days, girls may sing songs answered by the boys who may sing the same song with opposing, responding or parallel meanings given to partially improvised verses. All work on their poems in advance, but still sing them rather spontaneously at competitions scheduled during the festivals. *Quan họ* participants dress in their finest and most traditional costumes representing their villages, and throughout the days of preparation and lively competition seize the opportunity to build friendships with singers from near and far.

"Qua Cầu Gió Bay" is well known because it is a popular piece for live stage performances as well as recorded and broadcast versions. Each song presentation varies depending upon the context of the performance. The antiphonal (call-and-response) style, however, remains intact. The singers identify by turns a different piece of wearing apparel that has been blown away by the wind (shoes, scarf, gloves, shirt, hat, ring etc.).

Transcription: Thanh-Tuyen Ton-Nu

Translation:

1. Loving you I give you my coat. *(lit.: shirt)*
Coming back home I lie to father and mother:
On the bridge, the wind has taken it away.

2. Loving you I give you my hat.
Coming back home I lie to father and mother:
On the bridge, the wind has taken it away.

3. Loving you I give you my ring.
Coming back home I lie to father and mother:
On the bridge, because of the wind, it has dropped into the river.

Words and Pronunciation:

1. Yêu nhau cởi áo ý a cho nhau.
    (Ee-ew nya-oo ker-ee ao ee ah tsaw nya-oo.)
Về nhà dối rằng cha dối mẹ a ý a.
    (Vay nyah zoh-ee zang tsah zoh-ee mae ah ee ah.)
Rằng a ý a qua cầu. Rằng a ý a qua cầu.
    (Zang ah ee ah kwa ka-oo.)

    Chorus: Tình tình tình gió bay.
        (Ting ting ting zaw bay-ee.)
      Tình tình tình gió bay.

2. Yêu nhau cởi nón ý a cho nhau.
    (Ee-ew nya-oo ker-ee nawn ee ah tsaw nya-oo.)
Về nhà dối rằng cha dối mẹ a ý a.
    (Vay nyah zoh-ee zang tsah zoh-ee mae ah ee ah.)
Rằng a ý a qua cầu. Rằng a ý a qua cầu.
(Zang ah ee ah kwa ka-oo.)

    Chorus.

3. Yêu nhau cởi nhẫn ý a cho nhau.
    (Ee-ew nya-oo ker-ee nyern ee ah tsaw nya-oo.)
Về nhà dối rằng cha dối mẹ a ý a.
    (Vay nyah zoh-ee zang tsah zoh-ee mae ah ee ah.)
Rằng a ý a qua cầu. Rằng a ý a qua cầu.
    (Zang ah ee ah kwa ka-oo.)

    Final Chorus: Tình tình tình gió bay.
        (Ting ting ting zaw bay-ee.)
      Tình tình tình đánh rơi.
        (Ting ting ting dah-n zer-ee.)

Study Guide

Teaching/Learning Sequence   **Level: Grade 4 to Adult**

1. Discuss the custom of *quan họ* singing.
Focus particularly on the musical and social importance of this tradition. Why might it be important for young people of different villages to get together in this way? Singing and music competitions occur in many cultures, including those in the West. Compare the *quan họ* singing contests to others your group might be familiar with, for example, school music festivals, battles of the bands (marching bands, rock/pop, Dixieland, bag-pipes, steel drum or "pan" ensembles, blue grass etc.), "name that tune" games in the classroom or on television, or international piano competitions.

  • Do the words indicate anything about the relationship of young people to each other and/or to their parents in traditional Vietnamese society? Why do you think the singer feels the need to "lie to father and mother" about what happened to the apparel?

2. Listen to the recording:
  • *Are there any repetitions in this music?* (Yes: the text is the same in all verses except for one word, and the last two phrases repeat in each verse.)
  • *At the entrance of the chorus on the last phrase ("Tỉnh tỉnh"), clap the rhythm :*

  • *Step the pulse.* Change directions on the last phrase, while also clapping the rhythm.

3. Prepare to sing the song:
  • *Sing exercise #5* the natural minor scale, moving upward and downward, in dyads, and at different tempi. Use solfege or "la."

La Ti Do Re   Mi Fa Sol La   Sol Fa Mi Re   Do Ti La

La Ti Ti Do Do Re Re Mi   Mi Fa Fa Sol Sol La La Sol

Sol Fa Fa Mi Mi Re Re Do   Do Ti Ti La

Exercise 5
  • *Rhythmically pronounce the words of the phrases.*
  • *Say the last phrase twice,* while clapping its rhythm.

4. Sing the song:
  • *Sing the last phrase twice,* while clapping its rhythm.
  • *Sing the first phrases,* and add the last for the complete song.
  • *Choose a small group to sing the first section,* while a larger group sings the last phrase.

5. Compose a dance:
  • *Create a gentle wind-song dance* to reflect the mood and the text of the song, and the changing and repeated phrases. Like the music, the last two phrases that repeat themselves should be reflected in the movement.

VII. Đò Dọc Đò Ngang

"The Boat Song"

There are two kinds of boats commonly used on rivers in South Vietnam where I lived. One goes from one city to another place—that is the current flowing boat—and on the same body of water you will find another kind that takes people from this side to the other side of the river—that is a crossing boat. Many are very long and narrow in design to make it easier to flow quickly along with the current. They are stretched out so there is plenty of room to carry many things. This song is like many of the boat songs, in that it describes a kind of dualism: a man and a woman, this type of boat and that, different ways of rowing and different directions. But they sing about union, or unification, and ask why can't their wish of being united come true? In a way it presents a gentle plea to look past differences and see the ways we can be joined instead.

South of Saigon (now Ho Chi Minh City), the Mekong River delta of South Vietnam is washed by a system of rivers, both large and small. The Mekong and numerous other rivers make for a fertile agricultural region. River fishing and the cultivation of rice paddies are important economic mainstays for the people of this region. People use small boats called *đò* as their main means of transportation in the region, for these rivers are their roads. Songs sung on boats are composed or improvised by the peasants, and are based in large part on their folk poetry. These traditional poems contain riddles, comparison statements, and descriptions of nature.

As the boatmen and boatwomen row their boats along with the current, they sing to each other, teasing, developing friendships, and singing songs that test the boater's knowledge. Some of the songs focus on the topic of making friends along the river, and ask the way to a village or a particular home. And as with workers accompanied by sea shanties or African or American Indian paddling chants, field hollers, chain gang chants or a drill cadences, or the rhythmic rhymes of the coxswain on a crew team, the rowers may also find their songs help them work more efficiently and with less fatigue during a long trip. The words *"Khoan hỏi hò khoan"* sung at the endings of *"Đò Dọc Đò Ngang"* symbolize the sound of the water whirling about the paddle.

Transporting goods to market on the Ngoc Ho river where it passes in front of Phong Nguyen's house in South Vietnam. The riverboat is called *đò*.

Đò Dọc Đò Ngang

(daw yawk daw ngahng)

Refrain: Chorus:

(Khoan hởi hồ- o khoan Khoan khoan hởi hồ- o khoan.)
(k'wang haw-ee haw k'wang k'wang k'wang haw-ee haw k'wang.)

Soloist:
1. Em lái con đò-
Aem lah- ee kawng daw

ngang, anh sang con đò- dọc. Anh lái con đò- dọc, em trở con đò-
ngahng ahn shahng kawng daw yawk ahn lah- ee kawng daw yawk aem tr-er kawng daw

Chorus:
ngang. (Khoan hởi hồ- o khoan Khoan hởi hồ- o khoan.)
ngahng (K'wang haw-ee haw k'wang k'wang haw-ee haw k'wang

Verse: Soloist:
2. Mai ta một
Mah-ee tah moh

Chorus: **Soloist:**
dòng. (Khoan hởi hồ khoan) Sao không đồng lòng, mang tiếng hoài trông.
yawng k'wang haw-ee haw k'wang shah-o k'ohng dohng lawng mahng tee-eng hwai-ee trohng)

Translation:

Refrain/Chorus: *(The sound of water whirling about the paddle.)*

Verse 1:   *Girl: I row the crossing boat.*
       Boy: You row the current-flowing boat.
       Boy: You row the current-flowing boat.
       Girl: I row the crossing boat.

Verse 2:   Tomorrow we will get together in the same stream.
       Why shouldn't our wish come true?

Verse 3:   Listen to me this time: Tomorrow we will be dressed in pink.
       (Literally: "Tied in pink threads.")
       Why shouldn't we be married?

Verse 4:   We will be husband and wife.
       We will have many children and grandchildren.

Words and Pronunciation:

Refrain/Chorus: Khoan hởi hò khoan (2x)
(K'wang haw-ee haw k'wang)

Verse 1: Soloist: Em lái con đò ngang, anh sang con đò dọc.
(Aem lah-ee kawng daw ngahng ahn shahng kawng daw yawk)
Anh lái con đò dọc
(Ahn lah-ee kawng daw yawk)
Em trở con đò ngang.
(aem tr-er kawng daw ngahn)

Verse 2 : Soloist: Mai ta một dòng.
(mah-ee tah moh yawng)
Chorus: Khoan hởi hò khoan
(k'wang haw-ee haw k'wang)
Soloist: Sao không đồng lòng, mang tiếng hoài trông
(shah-oh k'ohng dohng lawng, mahng tee-eng hwai-ee trohng)

Verse 3: Soloist: Nghe anh một lần.
(ngae ahn moht learng)
Chorus: Khoan hởi hò khoan
Soloist: Ta xe chỉ hồng. Kết nghĩa được chăng?
(tah sae tsee hohng kay(t) ngee-ah dew(k) tsahng)
Chorus: Khoan hởi hò khoan, Khoan khoan hởi hò khoan
(k'wang haw-ee haw k'wang, k'wang k'wang haw-ee haw k'wang)

Verse 4: Soloist: Ta nên vợ chồng.
(tah nayng ver tsohng)
Chorus: Khoan hởi hò khoan
Soloist: Mai kia đầy đàn. Con cháu thiệt đông.
(mai-ee kee-ah day-ee dahng korn tsah-oo thiet dohng)
Chorus: Khoan hởi hò khoan, Khoan khoan hởi hò khoan
Soloist and chorus: Ta nên vợ chồng. Khoan hởi hò khoan.
(tah nayng ver tsohng, k'wang haw-ee haw k'wang)

Teaching/Learning Sequence   **Level: Grade 2 to Adult**

1. Locate the Mekong River on a map. Trace its course from the Tibetan highlands to the South China Sea, through the Southeast Asian countries of Thailand, Laos, and Cambodia to Vietnam.

    • Locate the Mekong River delta and name some of the other rivers that contribute to making this an important agricultural area.

2. Discuss the importance of the song to help alleviate the labor of paddling the boat. Work songs, as mentioned in the introduction, have been popular in many societies. "Michael, Row the Boat Ashore" is an example of a nineteenth-century Black American stevedore song. Today, "muzak" is piped into stores, offices and elevators and physical exercise is often accompanied by "work out" music. Talk about the various kinds of chants, hollers and songs used to accompany work in different cultures. Compare the themes found in other work songs to *"Đò Dọc Đò,"* for example love, overwork, hardship, the boss, misfortune etc.

3. Listen to the recording:
    • *Experiment with paddling movements.* Push the water away with the imaginary paddle. Paddle every four pulses; on the first beat only; every two pulses; alternating hands; with the entire arm; only with the fingers; in the rhythm of the chorus phrase:

    • *Paddle only on the "whirling water" response, "Khoan hởi hò khoan."* Remain still as the soloist sings.
    • *While listening to the recording, sing* the chorus together each time it occurs.

4. Prepare to sing.
    • *Sing exercise #6 .* The first half of the song (refrain) is based on a pentatonic scale (five-pitch), and the second half on a hexatonic scale (six-pitch). The *leader* sings the suggested tonal patterns, some of which are directly derived from the song, followed by *group* imitation. Patterns can be sung on "loo" or with solfege syllables.

Exercise 6

    • *Pronounce the phrases* of the soloist in the melodic rhythm.

5. Sing the song:
    • *Older groups might have a few singers try the solo part,* with the large chorus singing its prescribed phrase. Assign individual parts in the refrain, with the full ensemble singing the verses. *Younger groups sing only the refrain.*

VIII. Lý Tình Tang

"Song with 'Tình Tang' Endings"

I remember being in a certain friend's house in Saigon when I heard this on the radio. It is central Vietnamese, very hard to sing correctly if you were not born in the region, because of the Hue dialect, which is very particular. Certain gliding tones are very hard to imitate and central Vietnamese songs in general are hard to sing. The person on the tape is from central Vietnam. We sing the same words in the south, but with a different melody and scale. The chorus is made up of the names of musical notes. To many people these are nonsense syllables, but when you sing there is something very intimate that is felt, because they did originate in the folk tradition. In folksongs all throughout Vietnam you will find these words—they are very old. Nobody really knows where they came from originally.

"*Lý Tình Tang*" is an example of a song style of the Hue area of Central Vietnam. There are different texts possible for the *tình tang* style. In fact, any poem of six to eight syllables can be sung in this style, using the *tình tang* refrain. The poem used in this recording, "*Lý Con Sáo*" ("Song of the Blackbird") is probably the original poem first sung in this genre. Just as there are many poems that have been set in *tình tang* style, there are also many Vietnamese poems that have the same title, "*Lý Con Sáo*" ("Song of the Blackbird"), but which may use a different melody and style of singing. All of this may seem confusing, but the exchange of poems, melodies and singing styles typical of Vietnamese traditional music is illustrated through the origin and development of this song.

"*Lý Tình Tang*" was a folk song composed by peasants, simple and straightforward in its melodic patterns and at one time very quick in tempo. It gradually metamorphosed into art music performed by chamber ensembles of Hue. The listening tape presents the "Song of the Blackbird" as an example of the highly-evolved art song of Vietnam.

Three instruments and a women's chorus accompany this song: the *đàn tranh* zither, the *đàn bầu* monochord and the *song lang* or wood clapper. The sound of the monochord with its harmonics is blended into the music, offering a contrasting tone color to the metallic quality of the zither. It is the monochord which makes possible the delicate gliding tones of the accompaniment. Those not of the tradition who wish to perform this song authentically should attempt the difficult task of adjusting their voices slightly lower than the second and sixth degrees of the scale (i.e. about 20-30 Ellis cents lower than B and F#). Based on a common Vietnamese pentatonic scale, the flattening of notes produces for the informed listener a sweeter melody which consequently inspires a relaxed mood. Gliding tones of the song add to this effect.

Translation:

Who brought the blackbird to the other side of the river?
She will fly away when given the chance.

The mountain is high—who made it that high?
The ocean is so deep—who made it so deep?

Ly Tình Tang
(lee ting tahng)

↓ = sounds slightly lower;   ↑ = sounds slightly higher

Words and Pronunciation:

Soloist: Ai đem con sáo sang sông
(Ah-ee daem korn shao shahng shong)
Để cho, để cho con sáo
(Day tsaw day tsaw korn shao)
<u>*Chorus:*</u> Ố tang ố tang tình tang ơ Tình tang ơ tình, ố tang tình tang
(Oh tahng oh tahng ting tahng er ting tahng er ting oh tahng ting tahng)

Soloist: Xa bay xa tình là xa bay xa
(Sah bah-ee sah ting lah sah bah-ee sah)
<u>*Chorus:*</u> Ố tang ố tang tình tang ơ Tình tang ơ tình, ố tang tình tang

Soloist: Non cao ai đắp nên cao
(Nawng kah-oh eye dup nayn kah-oh)
Bể sâu, bể sâu nhờ bởi
(Bay-ee shau-oo bay-ee shau-oo nee-er ber-ee)
<u>*Chorus:*</u> Ố tang ố tang tình tang Ai...đào, ố tang tình tang
(Oh tahng oh tahng ting tahng eye dah-oh oh tahng ting tahng)

Soloist: Sâu bên sâu tình là sâu bên sâu
(shau-oo bayn shau-oo ting lah shau-oo bayn shau-oo)
<u>*Chorus:*</u> Ố tang ố tang tình tang. Tình tang... tình, ố tang tình tang

Teaching/Learning Sequence   Level: Grade 6 to Adult

1. Share your thoughts on the deeper meaning of the poem.

2. This song style uses various poems for the same melody. This is a common practice the world over. Members of the group might recall other examples from their traditions. For example, in the United States the folk song "Clementine" has been recast as the silly song, "I Found a Peanut;" "Cheerio," "Willowby," and "Zydeo" share some words and melody; and "On Top of Old Smokey " is parodied by "On Top of Spaghetti."

3. In Vietnam, different melodies are set to the same text. Compare the settings of the "Ave Maria" by Shubert and by Bach-Gounod. The Hebrew song "Shalom Chaverim" has been set to several melodies. Find others from various traditions.

4. Listen to the recording:
> • *The* song lang *(wood clapper) sounds a pulse every four beats.* Clap along with two fingers as the *song lang* plays.
> • *As one student plays the wood block with the* song lang *(beat 1), others patsch on beats 2, 3 and 4.*
> • Tap or clap the rhythm of the chorus section, "waving off" the rests.

5. Prepare to sing the song:
> • *Sing exercise #7.* The rhythmic scale-like exercise should be sung slowly on a neutral syllable while keeping the pulse. Sing the tonal patterns derived from the song, group members imitating the leader.

Exercise 7
> • *Pronounce each phrase of the chorus in its melodic rhythm.*

6. Sing the song:
> • Divide into two groups. As one group sings the chorus, the other steps the rhythm of the melody.
> • Sing the chorus together with the recording. Clap on the first beat, and patsch on beats 2, 3 and 4.

IX. Kim Tiền

"Golden Coin" or "Golden Fairy"

This is a piece I learned very quickly when I was ten. I had already heard and sung it, with other words, and therefore got used to the melody. My master asked me to play after him. He played the first phrase, then I repeated. Then the next, and I repeated that. Just like that. I liked it, and it was very easy to remember. The title is open for debate. If the words are said with a gliding tone at the end it means "Golden Coin," but the piece doesn't sound like coins at all! I found it in a 130-year-old book, in Sino-Vietnamese characters, and in this case it would not have had a gliding tone. The characters in the book mean "person" and "mountain." A person who lives on a mountain is a fairy. We do not have the original version of the words of the song – they are lost. Only the title remains. If we had the words we could tell, but there is a strong tradition of fairy tales, and I think the atmosphere and feeling in this piece has much more to do with fairies than coins!

"Kim Tiền" meaning Golden Coin or Golden Fairy, is one of the first musical pieces for beginning students of *đàn tranh* zither. *Đàn tranh* students usually begin serious study of instrumental music at the age of ten. "Kim Tiền" is a flavorful sixteenth-century melody of the chamber or court music genre, which originated in Central Vietnam. It is rather easy to remember, thanks to its repeated melodic structure utilizing A and B sections in various designs: AB/AB and ABA. This piece offers an experience in the monodic and ornamental character of Vietnamese traditional music.

In Vietnam, the performance of art music typically opens with an improvised prelude called *rao* or *dạo*. This prelude has many purposes: to ascertain the flexibility of strings, to check the tuning (or in some cases, the singer's voice), to prepare the mind for the mode (set of pitches) to be used, to create a particular mood within the ensemble of musicians, or to wait for the singer of the piece to begin. In an ensemble performance, the instruments play individual preludes one after another, followed by the full ensemble which plays the prelude together. The piece unfolds in this manner:

	Rao or dạo (prelude) *(Unmetered and improvised)*	**Piece** *(Metered and composed)*
Solo:	_____	_____
Ensemble:		
Instr. 1	____ _____	_____
Instr. 2	____ _____	_____
Instr. 3	_____ ____	_____

How is an instrumental piece learned? Consider the *đàn tranh* zither which performs "Kim Tiền" as a solo. As the featured instrument, the *đàn tranh* is tuned in a pentatonic arrangement, with three sets of five strings tuned in three successive octaves. The additional string (#16) serves the purpose of covering the whole three octave range. Each of the sixteen strings can be pushed downward with the left hand. This opens the possibility of not only altering a given pitch but of ornamenting it as well. The pitches are tuned to a range that is comfortable for the voice, as many of the pieces are vocal with instrumental accompaniment. The most common fundamental pitch is D above middle C.

The student plucks the strings of the *đàn tranh* with the right hand. Later, the ornamentation techniques are learned with the left hand. Ornamentation is essential to

Vietnamese music, regardless of genre, and is linked closely to the concept of mode. Vibrato (*rung*), staccato (*mõ*), and pushing (*nhấn*) are delicately applied as principal performance techniques for stringed instruments such as zither and lute, and the voice. Based on specific types of pentatonic, hexatonic, or heptatonic scales, these techniques must be employed in order to give each pitch its characteristic sound quality. Arpeggios and glissandos are also characteristic performance techniques for the *đàn tranh*. Without the ornamentation, a pitch may not be accurate in its sound as designated by the Vietnamese tradition. Ornamentation, as for this piece, is indicated in the score by the following symbols:

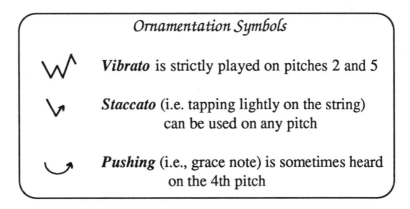

Ornamentation Symbols

Vibrato is strictly played on pitches 2 and 5

Staccato (i.e. tapping lightly on the string) can be used on any pitch

Pushing (i.e., grace note) is sometimes heard on the 4th pitch

In the Vietnamese tradition, music is performed in a half-improvised, half-composed manner. This means that the conventional notes at the strong beats are constantly maintained as the skeletal framework of the music. In the transcription of the piece, the conventional pitches found at even measures (i.e. 2, 4, 6, 8...) are marked with "x." These pitches sometimes anticipate the strong beat and are sounded just before it, or hesitate a bit and sound just after it. The syncopation produced by this technique is characteristic of instrumental music from central Vietnam.

Tuning of the Đàn Tranh for "Kim Tiền"															
1	2	3	4	5	6	7	8	9	10	11	12	13	14	15	16
D	E	G	A	B	d1	e1	g1	a1	b1	d2	e2	g2	a2	b2	d3

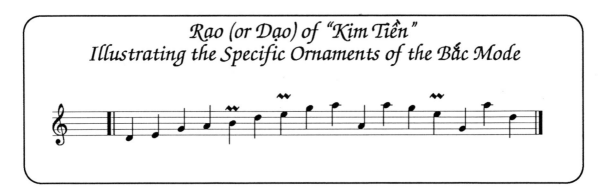

Rao (or Dạo) of "Kim Tiền"
Illustrating the Specific Ornaments of the Bắc Mode

Kim Tiền

Transcription of Đàn Tranh Performance by Phong Nguyen

Study Guide

Teaching/Learning Sequence   Level: Grade 4 - adult

1. **Discuss:**
   - *Discuss the use of the prelude in music.* Define its possible functions. Provide experiences with preludes in other music styles: the overture that precedes operas and musicals, the organ prelude before worship services, the "warm-up band" in a rock conert, the *alap* section in a performance by an Indian sitarist.
   - *Discuss the significance of ornamentation in music.* Find listening examples in the Baroque period of Western art music, Celtic folk songs, Black gospel music, and the blues. Demonstrate ornamentation vocally and on the piano or other instrument, including trills, glissandos, slides and ellisions, sustaining and anticipation tones.
   - *Discuss the importance of ornamentation in Vietnamese traditional music,* particularly on the *đàn tranh.*

2. **Listen to the recording: Keep in mind the development of the piece from the set of pitches to the prelude to the body of the piece.**

   - **There are three steps to realizing a piece on the *đàn tranh*: (Follow them on the tape.)**

   A. *The melody of the first two phrases is played in an unelaborate way.* Listen to
   [0:00-0:09]   the pentatonic tuning, and the plucking that is performed by the right hand.

   B. *An improvised prelude is played with both hands.* Listen for the vibrato, staccato,
   [0:10-0:31]   and grace notes.

   C. *The piece is played in an elaborate way.* All the possible performance techniques
   [0:32-1:56]   of the left and right hands are used for the *bắc* mode, which expresses a moderate happiness to the informed listener.

3. **Listen to the recording:**
   - *Play the pitches of the rao, and of phrase one and two, on recorder.*
     ~Sing the pitches. Listen for their ornamentation in the prelude.

   - *Follow the transcription* on a transparency, or with desk copies. Note the ornamentation of what appears at first to be a rather plain melody line.

X. Lý Ngựa Ô

"Song of the Black Horse"

I learned this from my father when I was ten and had started studying the stringed instruments. Because I knew how to sing the song already, it was not difficult to learn this quickly. In the folk version the rhythm is less syncopated and the melody is less embellished.

"*Lý Ngựa Ô*" is an example of chamber music from the south which originated in the folk tradition. The melody contains much syncopation, metabole (changes of scale within the piece), and decorative ways of playing two instruments in a heterophonic texture that features simultaneous variation.

"*Lý Ngựa Ô*" includes the *đàn tranh* zither and the *đàn nguyệt,* a moon-shaped long-necked lute. The *đàn nguyệt* plays a short improvised prelude that introduces its tone color, the pitches of the scale to be used throughout the piece, and the artist's individual embellishment techniques in the *bắc* mode. The *đàn tranh* zither enters with a musical question that is followed immediately by the *đàn nguyệt's* response. The two instruments then play together in a rhythmic and melodic counterpoint. The playing of two or more instruments stimulates improvisation within the framework of a piece. For listeners, the complex heterophony is quite removed from the monophonic work of "*Kim Tiền.*" The improvisation and heterophony are not really very free, however; they are controlled by the laws of the mode.

Big bell tower of Buddhist temple Than Quang Tu in Thai Binh province in northern Vietnam. Known commonly as *chùa Keo*, it is located in the area where the well known wise man and scholar of the 18th century, Le Quy Don lived. The complex architecture is very traditional. The temple is near the banks of a river, and the building and its grounds are used as a cultural center for the people. In addition to prayers, other activities including Buddhist chanting competition, music, art and even sporting events take place here.

Study Guide

Teaching/Learning Sequence

Level: Grade 4 - adult

1. Demonstrate heterophonic texture:
- *Sing "Yankee Doodle" while simultaneously playing a variation of it on the piano or other instrument.*
- *Lead the group in singing a familiar song ("He's Got the Whole World in His Hands," "Home on the Range," "Sandy Land," "Polly Wolly Doodle" etc.) while playing a variation of it on the piano.*

2. Listen to the recording.
- *Outline and call out these musical events as they occur:*
  - [1] Entrance of the *đàn nguyệt* brief improvised prelude.
  - [2] *Đàn tranh* musical question, with *song lang* (wooden clapper) entrance.
  - [3] *Đàn nguyệt* answer.
  - [4] Heterophonic duet of *đàn tranh* and *đàn nguyệt*.

- *Patsch or tap the* song lang *part, listening carefully for instances of syncopation.*

- *Write a poem or poetic phrase inspired by the music, but that relates to the song title: "Song of the Black Horse."*

A festival in a temple yard.

XI. The Voice of the Trống

The Tradition of Vietnamese Drumming

This is the easiest drum formula or pattern to learn. It is a basic pattern for ritual music ensembles, for the classical theater, for the shaman's dance, or in the Buddhist temple. I learned it from my master at the beginning of my percussion training at the age of seven.

"*Trống*" is the generic term for any kind of drum in Vietnamese music. The drumming tradition is exciting and energetic, and there are many different types of drums and drum pieces throughout Vietnam. Some of them play a leading role in ensembles and orchestras. An instrumental piece for the orchestra, for example, may begin and end only if the *trống* "engages" specific rhythmic formulae. A complicated method of elaborating rhythmic contours through improvisation is a remarkable feature of Vietnamese drumming.

Rhythm in Vietnamese music is a rather complex system. The taped example illustrates the basic rhythmic patterns of the two-headed drum or *trống* of the traditional ensemble used in village festivals. The cowskin surface of this drum measures 17 1/2 inches in diameter, and the wooden box of its body is 7 1/2 inches high. The *trống* stands on a square, foldable wooden stand about twenty inches high. The performer uses sticks to hit the drum on the skin heads and on the wooden body as well, utilizing open and damped strokes and presses. The heads may be hit at the center of the drum skin, or at the margin, which, combined with numerous types of strokes will produce a wide variety of sound qualities. To learn the drumming patterns, students chant mnemonic syllables in imitation of their teacher. This is also a common technique throughout Africa and India, and is used frequently by percussion teachers in the West as well—for students of rock and roll, swing or jazz drum set, high school marching band drum sections and drum corps. The syllables used, of course, vary from culture to culture, but the practice of verbalizing drum strokes fully before attempting to play them on the drums is widely known to be an effective preparatory step. The syllables used in Vietnamese drumming are shown below.

Vietnamese Drum Mnemonics

notation	type of stroke	spoken syllable
♩	at the center of the drum skin	*toong* (taw-ng)
♪	at the margin of the drum skin	*táng* (tah-ng)
♪	on the wooden box	*cắc* (kak)
♪	two sticks roll briefly and stop, pressing at the center of the skin	*rụp* (roop)
♪	right stick beats the center of the head while whole left stick presses on the skin	*tệch* (tay-k)

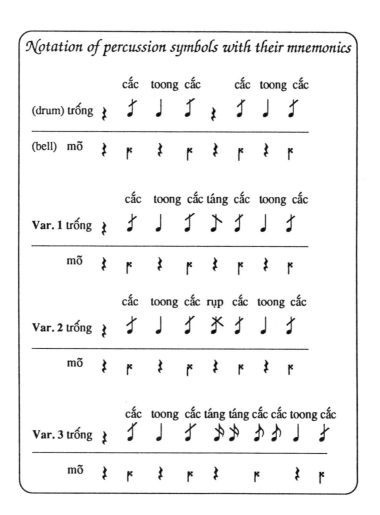

Notation of percussion symbols with their mnemonics

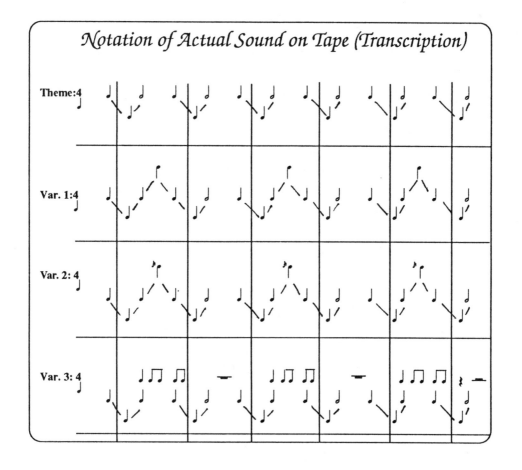

Notation of Actual Sound on Tape (Transcription)

Study Guide

Teaching/Learning Sequence   **Level: Grade 2 - adult**

1. Demonstrate the five drum strokes of the Vietnamese drum. Recite the mnemonic, followed by the stroke itself. Increase the number of strokes to eight or more.

Example:

Chant: cắc cắc cắc cắc cắc cắc cắc cắc

Play: ♪ ♪ ♪ ♪ ♪ ♪ ♪ ♪

(on margin of drum skin)

2. Using classroom drums, suggest the possible ways in which such instruments can be played to create the most variety of sounds. Substitute desks, table tops, plastic garbage pails, oatmeal boxes and pencil drum sticks, if necessary. Encourage group members to experiment.

- *Choose onomatopoeic syllables, or mnemonics, to represent the sound of the various drum strokes discovered.*

3. Listen to the recording:

In this drumming illustration, the composition is based on the 4-beat (2 weak, 2 strong) pattern in the first sequence. This is the most common in Vietnam in both folk and art music. The rhythmic cycle is doubled to 8 beats (4 weak, 4 strong) but in equal playing time and tempo in the rest of the sequences. Each example is played with only 11 strong beats; the first strong beat is omitted, leading to an emphasis on the second strong beat.

Note the additive nature of the piece, as various percussion instruments are played in the sequences.

- *Follow the notation of these sequences on the next page. The last percussion piece (about one minute in duration) is a full extension of possible rhythmic combinations.*

4. Chant the mnemonics of the drum theme and its three variations, as indicated in #3.

- *Following adequate practice, chant the mnemonic syllables along with the recording.*

5. As an extension of #2 participants may wish to compose and perform their own drum or percussion pieces.

- *Choose a percussion instrument and explore its sound possibilities.*
- *Assign mnemonic syllables to the sounds.*
- *Create a pattern of 8 to 24 beats or more of sound.*
- *Perform the piece, first chanting the mnemonics then playing it.*
- *Combine several instruments together for a polyrhythmic effect.*

XII. Chinh Phụ Ngâm Khúc

" The Song of A Soldier's Wife"

I learned the story in the poem when I was in high school in Saigon. I heard this version on radio and tape, and learned it by listening. There is freedom in improvising melody with a poem. I included this particular poem intentionally. Many Vietnamese people have been cut off from tradition because of the war and organization of the country now. It is my hope that this collection will reveal and nurture the mild character of the Vietnamese people, especially the young people who have lost our music and many of the traditions to a great extent.

"*Chinh Phụ Ngâm Khúc,*" "The Song of the Soldier's Wife," was composed by Dang Tran Con and Phan Huy Ich. Both were Vietnamese poets and scholars in the eighteenth century. Dang Tran Con, a mandarin nobleman under the Le dynasty, first wrote the legend in classical Chinese, while Phan Huy Ich, a much revered Doctor of Literature, translated the verses into the vernacular Vietnamese language. His 408 verses tell the tale through the voice of a wife, who laments the absence of her husband, who has been called to war for his country. The themes of the story-poem are the search for peace and the longing for a return to the simple joys of life prior to the advent of war.

Vietnamese storytelling is often heightened into a type of chant called *ngâm* (pronounced "nyah-m" and meaning "hymning," "chanting," or "singing"). Because of a melodious tonal language system, well-known legends and traditional stories are rhymed into poems that resemble songs when recited. A short story may have a hundred verses, while a long one contains more than eight thousand verses! The long stories require several nights of chanting in order to be completed; occasionally, particular sections are extracted from the larger legend for performance, as we have done on the companion tape. These legends may be historical, religious, social, educational, or mythical in nature.

The chant styles, their pitches and rhythms, vary from one region to the next. Traditional art music offers some of these styles, although some chant styles are specific to story-telling. There are three principal types of storytelling chant: *đọc thơ* (reading poems), *nói thơ* (speaking poems), and *ngâm thơ* (chanting poems). A good storyteller knows his or her expressive art: when and how to coordinate pitches, rhythms, and modes to the developments in the story. Two styles are demonstrated in the taped performance of the first section (twenty-four verse lines) of "The Song of a Soldier's Wife": *đọc thơ* and *ngâm thơ*. Even though Phuong Chi is reading the poem aloud, she is using a stylized elaboration of conversational speech to enhance communication of the mood and structure of the poem. The sung version flows seamlessly from the spoken, as the melody is clearly based on the intonation of speech and is not many steps from Phuong Chi 's fluidly recited version.

Chữ Hán
Classical Chinese Character

一. 凱時

1. 風塵

天地風塵
紅顏多屯.
悠悠彼蒼兮誰造因.
鼓聲動長安月.
5 烽火影照甘泉雲.
九重按劍起當席.
半夜飛檄傳將軍.
清平三百年天下.
從此武衣屬武臣.

2. 誓軍

10 伏里天門催曉誓.
行人重法輕離別.
弓箭兮在腰.
妻孥兮別袂.
獵獵旌旗兮出塞愁.
11 喧喧簫鼓兮辭家怨.
有怨兮分攜.
有愁兮契闊.

3. 男兒志

良人二十吳門豪.
投筆硯兮事弓刀.
16 直把連城獻明聖.
願將尺劍斬天驕.
丈夫千里志馬革.
泰山一擲輕鴻毛.
便辭閨閫俟征戰.

Chữ Nôm
Old Vietnamese Character

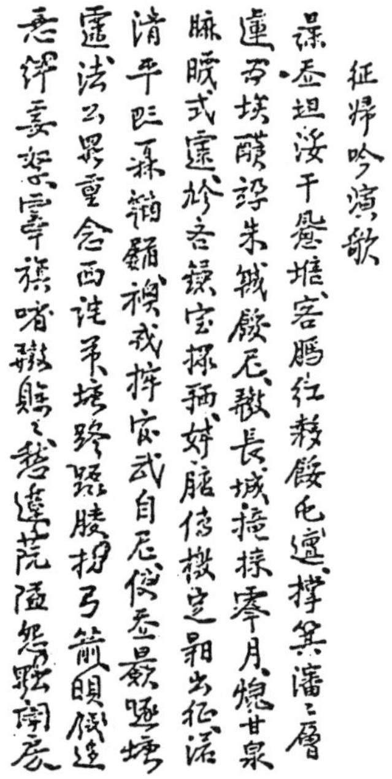

（征婦吟演歌 and vertical Nôm text columns）

Chữ Quốc Ngữ
Romanized Character

1. Thuở trời đất nổi cơn gió bụi,
   Khách má hồng nhiều nỗi truân chuyên.
   Xanh kia thăm thẳm từng trên !
   Vì ai gây dựng cho nên nỗi này ?

5. Trống Tràng thành lung lay bóng nguyệt,
   Khói Cam tuyền mở mịt thức mây,
   Chín tầng gươm báu trao tay,
   Nửa đêm truyền hịch định ngày xuất chinh.

   Nước thanh bình ba trăm năm cũ,
10. Áo nhung trao quan vũ từ đây,
    Sứ trời sớm giục đường mây,
    Phép công là trọng, niềm tây sá nào.

    Đường giong ruổi lưng đeo cung tiễn
    Buổi tiễn đưa lòng bận thê noa
15. Bóng cờ, tiếng trống xa xa,
    Sầu lên ngọn ải, oán ra cửa phòng.

    Chàng tuổi trẻ vốn giòng hào kiệt
    Xếp bút nghiên theo việc đao cung,
    Thành liền mong tiến bệ Rồng,
20. Thước gươm đã quyết chẳng dung giặc trời.

    Chí làm trai dặm nghìn da ngựa,
    Gieo Thái Sơn nhẹ tựa hồng mao.
    Giã nhà, đeo bức chiến bào,
    Thét roi cầu Vị, ào ào gió thu.

English

When all through earth and heaven rise dust storms,
how hard and rough, the road a woman walks!
O thou that rulest in yonder blue above,
who is the cause and maker of this woe?

In our Ch'ang-an drums beat and moonlight throbs.
On Mount Kan-ch'uan first burn and clouds glow red.
The Emperor, leaning on his precious sword,
at midnight calls for war and sets the day.

The realm has known three hundred years of peace—
now soldiers don their battle dress once more.
At daybreak heralds speed them through the mists—
the law outweighs what they may feel inside.

Full armed with bows and arrows, they fare forth,
from wives and children wrenching their numb hearts.
As banners wave and drums resound far off,
grief spreads from chamber door to mountain pass.

Born to a race of heroes, you my love,
discard your brush and ink for tools of war.
You vow to capture citadels for the throne—
your sword will spare no foe of Heaven's sway.

A man will win a horseskin for his shroud—
his life he'll drop in battle like goose down.
In war attire you leave and cross the Wei,
cracking your whip while roars the autumn wind.

[Translated by Huỳnh Sanh Thông, The Song of A Soldier's Wife (New Haven: Yale Center for International and Area Studies, 1986) reprinted by permission]

Study Guide

Teaching/Learning Sequence   **Level: Grade 2 to Adult**

---

1. Read the translation of the first section of the "Song of the Soldier's Wife."
  - What is the theme of the story-poem?

2. Listen to the recording:
  - *Note the different performance versions of the poem.*
  - *How are they different?*
  - *Listen for the connection between the spoken and the sung versions. Does English ever have a tonal quality? (Think of inflections for questions, children's playground chants, names, street vendor's cries.)*

3. Discuss the importance of stories in people's lives, as lessons for learning about the past, about people, and their relationships with others.
  - *When do stories become moral parables?*
  - *Orally transmitted stories are an important part of childhood in many cultures.* What stories do the members of the group recall? Who were the story tellers?
  - *What elements contribute to making storytelling an art form?*

5. Take turns reading a Vietnamese folktale, for example, "The Fisherman and the Goblet" (see bibliography).
  - *Demonstrate the ways in which the story can come alive* through the art of storytelling, by using vocal inflection, dynamics, and tempo changes to illustrate the text (high/low, loud/soft, fast/slow, gravelly-throated, etc.).
  - *As a long-term project, challenge group members to select, read and re-read a story,* and to arrive at a personal but dramatic way of telling it. The text need not be memorized, but the main characters and themes should come forward through the animation of the storyteller.

Kontum or Pleiku 1969, Pleiku Province.

Glossary

[Note: for precise pronunciation, check the guide at the beginning of the book, and the chart of how diacritical marks govern gliding tones. Otherwise, reading the words as they appear phonetically, as if they have no accent marks, results in a good approximation.]

Áo dài:	*the traditional long dress of men and women*
Áo tứ thân:	*four piece dress worn when girls sing folk songs in Bac Ninh province, North Vietnam or during village festivals.*
Ca Huế:	*Central Chamber Music*
Chập chõa:	*pair of cymbals*
Chiêng:	*gong*
Chữ quốc ngữ:	*the official written language of Vietnam, incorporating elements of Portuguese, Italian, and Greek elements, and using a system of romanized characters and diacritical markings (accent marks).*
Chùa:	*Buddhist temple*
Đại cổ:	*big temple drum*
Dân Ca:	*folk Songs*
Đàn bầu or đàn độc huyền:	*a monochord.*
Đàn đáy:	*a trapezoidal back-less lute.*
Đàn đoản:	*a short-necked, moon-shaped lute.*
Đàn gáo:	*a two-stringed coconut shell fiddle.*
Đàn nguyệt:	*a long necked moon-shaped lute.*
Đàn nhị:	*a two-stringed fiddle.*
Đàn tam:	*a three-stringed fretless lute.*
Đàn tam thập lục:	*hammered dulcimer*
Đàn t'rưng:	*xylophone, slung like a hammock on a frame. The bamboo tubes have holes in the bottom, some short, some long.*
Đàn tranh:	*a sixteen- or seventeen-stringed zither.*
Đàn tỳ bà:	*a pear-shaped lute.*
Đàn xến:	*an octagonal lute.*
Dạo:	*improvised prelude; see:* Rao
Diacritical marks:	*accent marks that indicate tonality in spoken Vietnamese.*
Đình:	*village temple or community center with an altar inside where some ritual ceremonies take place*
Đò:	*a common type of riverboat, long and narrow*
Hải loa:	*conch shell*
Hát Ả Đào:	*Northern chamber music*
Hát bội:	*classical theater performance*
Hát Cải Lương:	*Southern reformed theater*

Hát Chèo:	*Northern folk theater*
Hát Quan Họ:	*type of antiphonal group singing found near Hanoi*
Khăn đóng:	*hat made of silk cloth and worn on special occasions.*
Kèn:	*double-reed oboe*
Lễ Nhạc Phật Giáo:	*Buddhist Liturgy*
M'buat:	*mouth organ*
Mõ:	*wooden or bamboo bell*
Nhạc Tài Tử:	*Southern chamber Music*
Rao:	*unmetered, improvised prelude that typically opens a performance of art music*
Sáo:	*a transverse bamboo flute.*
Sinh tiền:	*coin clapper*
Song lang:	*foot clapper.*
Tân Nhạc:	*modernized vocal music*
Tết:	*one of the most ancient festivals, taking place during the lunar New Year, when people return to their birth place and family, visit tombs of ancestors, pay debts, pray.*
Tiêu:	*vertical flute*
Tonality:	*the gliding motion upward, dropping downward, or remaining on a certain pitch or tone of the voice when speaking Vietnamese.*
Trống:	*drum*
Trưng:	*bamboo xylophone, played by the Bahnar, an ethnic people of the Central Highlands. It is slung like a hammock on a frame. The bamboo tubes have holes of varying lengths along the bottom.*

Guide to the Companion Tape

Side A: Songs   Accompaniment   Duration

		Accompaniment	Duration
I:	*Hát Đúm*	none	00:26
	Chorus		
II:	*Cùm Nụm Cùm Nịu*	none	00:26
	Chorus		
III:	*Xây Khăn*	none	00:22
	Chorus		
IV:	*Cò Lã*	*zither and monochord*	05:59
	Phong Nguyen & Chorus	Phong Nguyen	
V:	*Lý Chim Quyên*	*zither*	01:40
	Thu Van & Chorus	Phong Nguyen	
VI:	*Qua Cầu Gió Bay*	*zither*	01:47
	Phong Nguyen, Tinh Trang	Phong Nguyen	
	& Chorus		
VII:	*Đò Dọc Đò Ngang*	*zither*	02:32
	Thu Van & Chorus	Phong Nguyen	
VIII:	*Lý Tình Tang*	*zither & monochord*	02:18
	Tinh Trang & Chorus	Phong Nguyen	

Side B: Instrumental Selections

IX:	*Kim Tiên*	*zither*	01:56
		Phong Nguyen	
X:	*Lý Ngựa Ô*	*zither & lute*	01:09
		Phong Nguyen	
XI:	Voice of the *Trống*	*drum & wooden bell*	01:50
		Phong Nguyen & Thu Van	

Poetry

XII:	*Chinh Phụ Ngâm Khúc*	*zither*	10:10
		Phuong Chi and Phong Nguyen	

The Performers
Soloists: Phong Nguyen, Thu Van, Tinh Trang, Phuong Chi
Chorus: Huong Lan, Kim Van, Kim Thanh, Mong Tuyet, Thu Van and Tinh Trang

The Instruments
Đàn bầu, monochord; *Đàn Nguyệt,* moon shaped lute; *Đàn Tranh,* 16 or 17-stringed zither; *Mõ,* wooden bell; *Trống,* drum.

(Recorded at Trax Recording, Seattle WA)

Bibliography

(J) = Juvenile

Addis, Stephen
    "Theatre Music of Vietnam," in *Southeast Asian Journal,* Vol. 1:1-2, 1971.

Buttinger, Joseph
    The Smaller Dragon. NY: Praeger Press, 1958.

Campbell, Patricia Shehan
    Sounds of the World: Music of Southeast Asia: Lao, Hmong, and Vietnamese.
    Reston, VA: Music Educators National Conference, 1986.

(J) Cole, Joanna
    Best Loved Folk Tales. Garden City, NY: Doubleday, Anchor Press, 1983.

Crawford, Ann
    Customs and Culture of Vietnam. Rutland, VT: C. E. Tuttle Co., 1966.

Dang, Tran Con & Huy Ich Phan
    The Song Of A Soldier's Wife. Trans: Huynh Sanh Thong. New Haven: Yale Southeast
    Asia Studies, 1986.

Dang, Van Lung, Thao Hong & Linh Quy Tran
    Quan Ho -- Nguon Goc va Qua Trinh Phat Trien (Quan Ho Folk Songs: Origin and
    Development). Hanoi: Khoa Hoc Xa Hôi, 1978.

Dao, Duy Anh
    Viet Nam Van Hoa Su Cuong (A Brief History of Vietnamese Culture). Hanoi: Quan
    Hai Tung Thu, 1938.

Doyle, Edward, Samuel Lipsman and the editors of Boston Publishing Company
    The Vietnam Experience (Setting the Stage). Boston: Boston Pub. Co., 1981

Durand, Maurice & Pierre Huard
    Connaissance du Vietnam (Understanding Vietnam).Paris:Imprimerie Nationale, 1954.

Groslier, Bernard
    The Art of Indochina. NY: Crown Publishers, 1962.

Hammer, Ellen Jay
    Vietnam, Yesterday and Today. NY: Holt, Rinehart & Winston, 1966.

Karnow, Stanley
    Vietnam: A History. NY: Penguin, 1984.

Le, Giang, Nhat Vu Lu, Van Hoa Nguyen & Luan Minh
Dan Ca Hau Giang (Folk Songs of Mekong Delta). Hau Giang: Ty Van Hoa va Thong Tin. 1986.

Lu, Nhat Vu & Giang Le
Dan Ca Ben Tre (Folk Songs of Ben Tre). Ben Tre: Ty Van Hoa va Thong Tin. 1981.

Ly, Te Xuyen
Viet Dien U Linh (ancient book).

Nguyen, Hien Le & Van Chinh Truong
Khao Luan Ve Ngu Phap Viet Nam (A Study of Vietnamese Gramatical Rules). Hue: University of Hue, 1963.

Nguyen, Huu Ba
Dan Ca Viet Nam - Folk Songs. Saigon: Ministry of Education, 1970.

Nguyen, Khac Kham
An Introduction to Vietnamese Culture. Tokyo: Center for East-Asian Cultural Studies, 1967.

Nguyen, Ngoc Bich
A Thousand Years of Vietnamese Poetry. NY: Alfred A. Knopf, 1975.

Nguyen, Thuyet Phong
The Gioi Am Thanh Viet Nam (The World of Vietnamese Music). San Jose: Hoa Cau, 1989.

_____"Dan Ca Viet Nam: Cac The Loai Thong Dung," (Vietnamese Folk Songs:Well-known Styles) in *Dat Moi* 4/15 (1986):14 & 30.

_____"Music in Exile: Music of the Vietnamese Immigrants in the United States." NY: World Music Institute: The New Americans Series, 1989.

_____"Music of the Vietnamese Immigrants of the United States: An Assessment of Genres and Performers." Social Science Research Council Report, 1989.

_____"Restructuring the Fixed Pitches of the Vietnamese Dan Nguyet Lute: A Modification Necessitated by the Modal System." in *Asian Music* 18/1(1986): 56-70.

_____"Une Esquisse de la Tradition Musicale du Vietnam," (A Sketch of the Musical Tradition of Vietnam), in *The Vietnam Forum* 1 (1983): 67-69.

(J) Poole, Frederick Kin
Southeast Asia. NY: Franklin Watts, Inc., 1972.

Pham, Duy

  Dan Ca / Folk Songs. Saigon: Melody Trails, 1966.

  _____*Musics of Vietnam.* Carbondale, Ill: Southern Illinois University Press, 1975.

Schultz, George F.

  Vietnamese Legends. Rutland, VT: C.E. Tuttle Co., 1965.

Sadie, Stanley, ed.

  New Grove Dictionary of Music and Musicians. London: Macmillan, 1980.

Taylor, Keith Weller

  The Birth of Vietnam. Berkeley-Los Angeles-London: University of California Press, 1983.

(J) Taylor, Mark

  The Fisherman and the Goblet: A Vietnamese Folk Tale. San Carlos, CA: Golden Gate Junior Books, 1971.

Toan, Anh

  Hoi He Dinh Dam (Traditional Festivals and Rituals). Saigon: Nam Chi Tung Thu, 1969.

Tran, Huu Phap

  Dan Ca Dong Bang Bac Bo (Folk Songs of the Northern Plains). Hanoi, 1961.

Tran, Van Khai

  Nghe Thuat San Khau Viet Nam (Theatrical Art of Vietnam). Saigon: Khai Tri, 1970.

Tran, Van Khe

  Einfuhrung in die Musik Vietnams (An Introduction to Vietnamese Music). Trans. Gisela Kiehl. Wilhelmshaven: Heinrichshofen, 1982.

Van, Giang

  The Vietnamese Traditional Music. Saigon: Ministry of Cultural Affaires. sd.

Recordings

(Records and Cassettes)

Chau Van Possession Chant from Vietnam. World Music Enterprises WME112, Kent, Ohio (cassette).

Instrumental Music of Vietnam: Dan Tranh. World Music Enterprises WME1007. Kent, Ohio (cassette).

Music from North and South Vietnam. Folkways AHM 4219.

Music of Southeast Asia: Lao, Hmong, and Vietnamese (Sounds of the World series). Music Educators National Conference, 1986. Three tapes of performances of southeast Asian musicians in the U.S., with interviews. Teaching guide by Patricia Shehan Campbell.

Music of Vietnam. World Music Enterprises WME110, Kent, Ohio (a set of 4 cassettes).

Music of Vietnam: The Phong Nguyen Ensemble. World Music Institute WMI 008, New York, (cassette).

Music of Vietnam. Lyrichord LLST 7337.

Musical Theatre of Vietnam: Hat Cheo, Hat Boi, and Cai Luong. World Music Enterprises WME111, Kent, Ohio (cassette).

Musique du Vietnam: Tradition du Sud. OCORA OCR68. Paris (disc).

Musique Mnong Gar - Vietnam. OCORA OCR 80. Paris (disc).

Traditional Music of Vietnam. Lyrichord LLST 7396. New York.

Tuong Nho Hon Que (Thinking of the Home Land). Van Hong VH001 (cassette).

Vietnam I: The Tradition of Hue. UNESCO Collection. Musicaphon BM 30L2022. Kassel - Basel - Paris (disc).

Vietnam II: Southern Tradition. UNESCO Collection. Musicaphon BM 30L2023. Kassel - Basel - Paris (disc).

Vietnamese Music in France and the United States. World Music Enterprises WME 1008. Kent, Ohio (cassette).

Filmography

Lan va Diep (Lan and Diep). THVN 9 / Art Studio. Santa Ana, California (video).

Mekong. 25 minutes, color. Produced by Shell Oil, 1970. Available AVLS, 3300 University Southeast, Minneapolis, MN 55414. Grades 4-9. Study of the Mekong River that spans Thailand, Cambodia, Laos and Vietnam, and problems related to its course and habits.

Tieng Hac Trong Trang (Song of the Crane in the Moonlight). Hoa Tinh Thuong 2-1983 (video).

Traditional Instrumental and Vocal Music of Vietnam: Dr. Nguyen Thuyet Phong in Discussion and Performance. Kent State University's Center for the Study of World Musics. CSWM 001. Kent, Ohio (60 min. video).

Index